EMPATH

THE PRACTICAL SURVIVAL GUIDE FOR EMPATHS
AND HIGHLY SENSITIVE PEOPLE TO HEALING
THEMSELVES AND THRIVING IN THEIR LIVES,
EVEN IF YOU CONSTANTLY ABSORB NEGATIVE
ENERGY AND ALWAYS FEEL DRAINED

JESSICA FLOWERS

CONTENTS

Introduction — v

1. What Does It Mean To Be an Empath — 1
2. Two Sides of an Empath's Coin — 50
3. Are You an Empath or Just Being Empathic? — 68
4. The Empath's Own Problems and Struggles — 80
5. Stay Empathic Without Burning Out — 102
6. Relationships, Career and World Transformation — 144

Afterword — 153
References — 157

© **Copyright 2020 - All rights reserved.**

The content contained within this book may not be reproduced, duplicated or transmitted without direct written permission from the author or the publisher.

Under no circumstances will any blame or legal responsibility be held against the publisher, or author, for any damages, reparation, or monetary loss due to the information contained within this book; either directly or indirectly.

Legal Notice:

This book is copyright protected. This book is only for personal use. You cannot amend, distribute, sell, use, quote or paraphrase any part, or the content within this book, without the consent of the author or publisher.

Disclaimer Notice:

Please note the information contained within this document is for educational and entertainment purposes only. All effort has been executed to present accurate, up to date, and reliable, complete information. No warranties of any kind are declared or implied. Readers acknowledge that the author is not engaging in the rendering of legal, financial, medical or professional advice.

INTRODUCTION

Empathy is a beautiful gift. Yet, the world can often be a cold and harsh place. People judge, misperceive, abuse and slander. There are such things as toxic characters, narcissists and energy vampires who see the sweet and unconditionally giving gifts of an empath, and seek to take. There are also highly manipulative and abusive characters who have no problem destroying an empath's trust or acting primarily selfishly, regardless of how selfless and sincere one's empathy is. In short, being an empath is an extraordinary and unique experience in itself, providing you can learn to master the journey and ride the waves.

So, to first understand the topic in question we must define our understanding of empathy and what it means to be an empath. Empathy is the ability to know what it is like to be in another's shoes. To have empathy is to know, sense, feel and "tune into" hidden emotions, feelings, thoughts and subtle influences or intentions. More so, empathy is the gift of compassion combined with feeling and uses senses beyond the five physical senses. An empath takes this ability to a whole new level. Empaths can literally merge with someone to the point of experiencing their world, or reality, as if it is theirs. The other person's thoughts become their thoughts, their emotions become their emotions, and virtually any and all sensation or inner impulse is felt and experienced on a real and intimate level. Now, it may be obvious at this stage that this can be both a gift and a blessing, or a curse! The experience of being an empath all depends on one's ability to stay strong and centered within healthy *boundaries*, protected in their truth and self- alignment and further at ease with their own highly sensitive nature; or unprotected, misaligned and lacking all boundaries.

If the latter is the case, one can become so disoriented picking up on everyone's thoughts, feelings and subte intentions or impressions, that other people's negative energy ("negative vibes!") are all they know. For this reason alone it is highly important to become aware of what it actually means to be an empath, and further seek to strengthen, protect and cherish the beautiful gifts and intentions that accompany. Quite simply, not everyone is on the same wavelength and accepting this is the first step to succeeding as an empath or highly sensitive person (HSP).

This book will serve as a practical guide on how to harness the gift of being an empath and thrive in this modern world, without burning out and also achieving health, happiness and personal success.

WHAT DOES IT MEAN TO BE AN EMPATH

DEFINING EMPATHY

We have briefly defined empathy in the introduction, but being an empath is a complex and deeply holistic and integrated experience. If you are an empath- and we are assuming you are as you are choosing to read this book!- you are wise, caring, compassionate, insightful and perceptive. You take care of those you love and have a deep consideration and respect for all life on earth, including animals, plant species, and the natural world, and of course, fellow humans.

It is important when looking into how you can live your best life and thrive psychologically, mentally, emotionally, physically, and spiritually that you first have a sound *inner*standing of what it truly means to be an empath. There are different levels to being an empath, as we will explore in the next section; however, for now, let's break down the empath personality so you can innerstand it holistically. Notice how understand has been adapted to innerstand, as this portrays the empath nature and personality in its prime. You possess unique skills in connecting to the inner depths, and inside realms and realities empaths often miss.

All of the following explorations are aspects to the empath personality in varying degrees. For example, you may resonate strongly with some, and with others, you may only see a small part of yourself embodying. As these chapters are intended to help you thrive and *heal on multiple levels,* it is important to explore these archetypes of yourself with an open mind and with higher awareness. This knowledge is not taught in school, nor is it widely accepted and many unique abilities that accompany being spiritually aware and connected and existing in a higher frequency or vibrational state of being are intuitively felt and under- innerstood. Your empath nature connects instinctively to something beyond the everyday 'I' and often separation based reality, which many people still reside in. Looking at the varying aspects to being an empath, therefore, can be a healing journey in itself. It is OK if you only resonate with a few- not all empaths display all of these qualities or characteristics. As you read the different aspects of the empath personality, shift your awareness back to memories or a memory where you may have been displaying some of these abilities without being conscious of what was occurring at the time. In the next section, there is a description of what it means, followed by how you may have been subconsciously or unconsciously displaying and embodying it. These are known as the *empath signs* and are closely linked in everything explored in Defining Empathy.

The Artist, Creative and Visionary

Firstly, you are an artist. You possess the unique ability to connect to some universal archetype, idea, concept, or image, also known as imagery or having vision, and can *tune in* to subtle thought forms and often ingenious ideas through this gift. Ideas and profound archetypal wisdom or imagery that others may not be able to access comes naturally to you, and with self- development and healing practices like meditation, sound therapy, spiritual healing, and energy work, you can amplify this natural gift of yours tenfold. Your ability to connect to something "above and beyond" you makes you a natural artist, creative and visionary, in short, and this is enhanced through your emotional and intuitive gifts. Oh yes, you are incredibly intuitive, so much so that your abilities often lie in the psychic and clairvoyant fields (more on this later!). Regarding your inner artist, however, you choose to express yourself; through song, dance, art, painting, drawing, poetry, writing, photography, film making, design, or creative directing. You can achieve great things. The visionary aspect of your nature can literally connect on an unseen and invisible level to some concept or archetype beyond the physical realm, further bringing it forth into the physical and material world. You perceive, see, and feel in a different way to non- empaths, and this makes you very gifted in the artistic realms. Alanis Morissette is one of the most well-known empaths, and even if you have not yet heard of her- her music inspires many people around the world.

The way you can excel and thrive in these areas of self- expression comes from your deep emotional and intuitive abilities, as briefly mentioned. As an empath, you are connected to an *advanced and evolved emotional frequency*, meaning that you operate and function on an advanced emotional frequency. You combine compassion with a strong sense of unconditional love and understanding (essentially- empathy), which allows you to attune to the subtle planes and dimensions of being. All thoughts, emotions, feelings, and beliefs arise from subtle energy. So do all mental constructs and virtually every aspect of consciousness that creates our individuality and thinking, feeling and interacting, or acting, existence. In other words, our emotions and thoughts arise from subconscious and subtle influences, and each specific thought, belief, or emotion holds its own unique vibratory frequency. Now, in terms of being an empath, for you, it is like walking into a room and instantaneously turning your awareness to all the plants in the room or to two people engaged in a deep, emotionally transparent, and authentic or affection conversation. Someone else may walk into the room and gravitate towards the duke- box blasting metal or rock, or automatically choose to sit with the gamers who are enticed in a reality of shooting people. You, dear empathic one, exist on a special frequency.

This is not saying you are better than anyone else, although- on a level- you are; because you have an evolved emotional understanding and are capable of advanced displays and genuine feelings of love and compassion, or simply care for your fellow human beings. Also, you do naturally gravitate towards higher things, your higher self, and your higher mind. (We explore this in-depth later.) But this mental image does intend to portray how you think, feel, and act and what you subconsciously respond to. Instead of choosing acts of war, violence, and hatred, represented through the shooting and killing spree, you choose human interaction symbolized by depth and authenticity. Instead of instinctively going towards the quite dark and heavy metal music, you are inclined to look towards the peaceful, life-giving, and divinely simplistic plants and greenery in the room. So in terms of your true nature being that of an artist, creative and visionary, hopefully, this analogy shows your gifts and capabilities. You attune- tune in- to frequencies and vibratory states of being in harmony with a certain "vibe," a reality of connection, emotional depth, and true harmony on the deepest of levels. You also share a natural affinity with nature and the natural world, therefore a *natural and pure frequency*. (What is purer than nature?)

This signifies that your mind wanders in unique

directions, which allow you to connect to abstract ideas, unseen concepts, and profound archetypal or subtle mental and emotional channels for creation. Think abstract, subconscious, subtle, and energetic.

The Musician, Performer and Storyteller

Like the artist, creative and visionary, you are a musician, performer, and storyteller. Actually, anything which enables you to connect to your self-expressive, creative, and imaginative self and mind brings out your inner empath. You are *deeply imaginative and self- expression*. You thrive in the Arts or any career or professional path (or hobby or pastime), which opens you up to new levels of imaginative thought and playful expression, and you further have a rare confidence to you that many would not have originally assumed. This is due to your noninvasive, receptive, and often passive nature. You may even appear shy, reserved, or down at times because you are so self-sacrificing and graceful in your mannerisms, intentions, and expressions. But this is what makes people love you and also what makes you shine in the Arts and musical, creative or acting-performing worlds. Others often perceive you as introverted, and many empaths certainly can be drawn to introverted tendencies, but they are not mutually exclusive. Being an empath is a highly extroverted and social experience, and this is because you thrive off of social connections and community or family ties. Quite simply, you are *introspectively-inclined* yet *social* with a love of deep emotional bonds, authentic friendships, and shared creative ventures or pursuits. Despite sometimes appearing as shy, quiet, soft-spoken, or reserved, you have a wild and highly passionate side which, when allowed to shine- can make you very inspiring.

Your ability to connect with unseen concepts and ideals, hidden emotions and impulses, inner instincts, and the vast array of the human experience makes you truly captivating and breathtaking. Furthermore, an empath fully stepped into their inspiring and motivating role is extremely confident and courageous- you literally have no fear! Emotions, personas, and expressions other people may be scared to show or fully embody, you can merge with to the point that anyone- including yourself- truly believes that you are that character or image- representation you are seeking to project. It is like you merge with another's essence and actually become that being, entity or character persona; and isn't this what makes a world-class actor, actress or performer? The same is true for music. Music to you is a transcendental and almost- mystic experience… you can express any emotion, frequency, concept or story through music, either through your voice, music production or an instrument; or dance. Whatever your tool and channel, you are extraordinarily gifted and many empaths don't even need excessive training or "lessons" to be able to do it. You have the ability to attain self-mastery and have mastered levels of skill and ability simply through your energy. Of course, if you do decide to choose a grounded path and go down the traditional route, dedicating your life to a talent, instrument or vocation will make you world-class and top in your field.

Your abilities in these realms stems from your belief in and desire for love. Love and the spirit of human connection fuels you, it motivates everything you do and every gift you possess. This love may be romantic, sexual, erotic, platonic, unviersal or all-encompassing, but it is always unconditonal and pure. Finding the strength and soul-power within you to connect to your empathic gifts and qualities fully will open new doors for you and steer you onto incredible musical performance-based inspirational paths, if you should so choose this route. Once you find yourself, become centered and begin to live in an empathic and harmonious flow, you will find that using your gifts and personality strengths through poetry, performing, storyteller or by connecting others through musical expression comes naturally to you, and can be a great gift for the world. Your empathy is inspirational!

The Dreamer, Seer and Psychic

One thing that is not often taught in schools nor accepted mainstream is the fact that you are an extremely gifted person. You are a dreamer- you love to explore your dreams and merge with other worlds and possess the natural capabilities to do so. Whereas some people need to spend years of training, attending numerous workshops, courses or retreats, or practicing lucid dreaming or astral projection for hours upon hours in their room, many empaths can do this naturally. It can actually be quite infuriating to some (trust me, I have a non-empath friend who spent thousands of pounds on lucid dreaming and astral projection retreats and workshops, and despite his intentions just could not do it!). Yet, to you it is as easy and effortless as breathing. Just like everything which was said with regards to you being an artist, creative and visionary; your ability to access invisible realms and attune to your subconscious mind is extraordinary. Truly extra-ordinary. It is in dreams where subconscious messages, insights, guidance and universal or collective archetypes and imagery are profound and can be accessed, and your empathic nature allows you to do so in the most advanced ways. Lucid dreaming is a form of "heightened or transcended consciousness" whereby your conscious mind is awake and aware in your dream. It is essentially a portal into the dream and subconscious world and realms, and instead of being unconscious, unaware and asleep, some aspect of your waking- life mind is present. Astral project is the ability of being conscious and present during a sort of meditation or meditative state, or place "in between dreams and waking life." Essentially, your mind is free to wander and explore consciousness and spiritual, mystical or subtle states of being whilst you are simultaneously connected to your body. The intention? To access your subconscious or some universal symbolism, archetype, insight or extraordinary new idea!

Furthermore, many empaths have a seer-like quality and essence to them. Psychic ability, intuitive sight, extrasensory perception and advanced spiritual or shamanic gifts are all common with empaths. The key to know is that empathy is having a deep emotional connection to someone to the point where you can feel what they are feeling. Yet empathy extends and expands beyond this, it is also having deep mental and spiritual bonds and being able to sense, feel and know what others are thinking. Knowing things without being told, being able to tell when someone is ill or what specific ailment they have, and being able to suss out beliefs and opinions without being told are all common. You can also instinctively sense what someone is about to say, or which direction the conversation is about to flow in. This is due to the nature of energy and being- we live in an energetic universe where subtle influences govern reality as we know it. This psychic sixth sense or seer-like ability arises from your deep emotional connection to others, yourself and the world, therefore you are in tune with the subconscious realm and the realms of emotion; which is where all thought, beliefs, perspectives and interactions arise. Are you starting to see the connection and whole picture? Good, we hope so.

So you can connect to some archetype or invisible symbol or idea which transcends this three-dimensional reality, and this makes you a natural dreamer, psychic and seer. Clairvoyance, clairaudience, clairsentience and claircognizance may all come naturally to you or you may have started consciously working with dreams in your teens. This means that whilst others were absorbed in other worlds and *frequencies* you were dreaming. There is a strong spiritual inclination to being an empath too, which we explore later.

Referring back to astral projection and lucid dreaming; we all have an astral body, an energetic layer of ourselves which extends beyond the physical. This astral layer of existence is responsible for all links and connections to psychic, intuitive, spiritual, and archetypal phenomena. It is also where you can connect to dream worlds and your subconscious during sleep or in that period between waking life and sleep when you are in between the worlds. *Astral travel* is the ability to explore some other dimension, dream scenario or altered state of consciousness at will, completely connected to your conscious mind. You vibrate at a different frequency- a higher frequency where- again- archetypes and subconscious messages or wisdoms are rich. This is all intrinsically linked to the higher self and higher mind which is an integral part to being an empath… you can tune into some higher power, divine or cosmic reality, or simply advanced channels of imaginative thought and expression.

The Healer, Counselor and Therapist

Linked to the last aspect of your nature and personality is the fact that you, dear empath, are a natural healer and counsellor. You have a deeply significant healing quality to you, and further may find yourself taking on a counselling role to those around you. Have you ever been sat on a public bench or stood in a natural spot in deep contemplation, and a total stranger has come up to you and started talking to you about their problems? Of course you have, and it's incredible. This is because of your heart, sincerity and soul... There is so much to say here and arguably this part of your empathic personality is a foundational one- i.e. it creates the basis of all of your other gifts, desires and abilities. So let's begin.

Because of your unique gifts of connecting to others on a deep level, and the genuine desire to do so, you are a natural healer. When referring to you having a "healing presence," this is literally because people come up to you to spill their deepest secrets or most sincere problems on you. They can feel something in your aura, your subtle but very real energy field, which says *I am compassionate, a great listener and genuinely care about your feelings. Please feel free to use my empathy to heal yourself and release your problems.* If your subtle energy field could speak, this is what it would say! In fact, many empaths go on to become healers or therapists as these paths and professions are strongly associated with your true nature. Your advanced and sincerely deep levels of empathy allow you to read minds, feel feelings, tune into emotions, and sense things without being told. This "reading of minds" is essentially a psychic gift and an enhanced intuition, an intuition so strong that you may be fully clairvoyant or capable of telepathy. Yet, you don't do so from a superficial or egotistical way, you do it because of a genuine desire and compassion to help and heal through your natural gifts. This is what makes you a true healer, at heart, and why you are the perfect counsellor, therapist of any kind or healer; if you should choose this route.

Combined with all of this is the truth that you are an extraordinary listener. It has already been stated that people may come up to you in the street or when in a quiet, zen or introspective space in public or at a social gathering, and start talking to you- usually with some problem or open- hearted speech about their life. But this further makes you extremely talented at any counselling or therapy role. Your unique ability to *hold space* for others is truly extraordinary. And you most likely don't need much training, or if you do you will feel like you already know it all and the teacher or trainer is like your own subconscious speaking back at you. Holding space is staying centered and aligned and maintaining your personal vibration whilst consciously choosing to direct the energy and flow of the conversation towards the other person's needs. This is ultimately unconditional love, compassion and empathy merged with warmth, an open heart and mind and a genuine desire to heal or help, through listening, understanding and a sense of selflessness. When you hold space you dedicate and devote your time, attention and energy solely to the person you are seeking to help; there is no selfish intentions or manipulative or hidden motives. You become a channel or conduit for the other person's healing journey and experience, and this is an extremely selfless and beautiful thing to do. Well, you do it naturally and often even when you don't know you're doing it. This is because of your true nature and subtle intentions, thus the empath nature and personality is one of the purest expressions of love any human could hope to achieve in a lifetime.

Quite simply, people feel comforted, safe and protected around you, and you tend to live and resonate in your *heart chakra.* Your heart chakra is known as the central chakra, the energy vortex which links lower self and higher self and is further the seat of compassion, kindness, empathy, and a connection to others and the natural world. Having a strong heart chakra enables you to thrive in any healing or counseling profession or simply to your friends and family.

The Carer, Social or Support Worker, and Companion

Connected to being a natural healer, counselor, and therapist is your innate tendencies and drive to take on a caring and supporting role. Many of the caregivers, social and support workers, and elderly or animal companions you see today are either empaths, or have strong empathic tendencies. You are one of the most selfless, genuine and giving souls and nothing is too much for you. You are happy to hold space for others, either loved ones or complete strangers, and are deeply caring and supportive in your energy, intentions and motivations. The definition of empathy is the ability to connect, merge and bond with another on a deep and emotional level, and this is one of your greatest strengths. Unlike "toxic" and selfish characters like narcissists and energy vampires, who thrive off of taking; you like to give. As an empath, you are deeply connected to your environments, surroundings and other people- or animals- so anything which threatens your connection can lead to pain, struggle, suffering and inner turmoil. Why, you may be wondering?

Because the whole reality of an empath is wrapped up in one's connection to others, therefore anything which seeks to diminish this connection and subsequently lead to disconnection or separation results in a significant loss of security, at least from a feeling-based level. In other words, your entire sense of security, safety and self-esteem is tied into the way you relate and interact with others. If someone attempts to break this it can create feelings of confusion, low self-worth and self-esteem and a questioning of your own beliefs, gifts, abilities and reality. As we explore later, this is why it is essential to protect yourself and develop healthy boundaries, especially against narcissistic characters and those who wish to abuse your kind and giving nature. It is also why channeling and expressing these qualities of yours can lead to you living your best, most happy and harmonious, and empathically attuned life.

The Animal Whisperer, Charity Worker and Volunteer

With everything expressed above this makes you an

excellent animal whisperer, charity worker and volunteer, or allows you to thrive in any role or activity which taps into your selfless, helping and highly compassionate-empathic nature. The empath personality is defined by connection, understanding (and now you are aware, *inner*standing), and being able to feel what it is like to be another. Many of you take this ability further and can actually read minds, or at least merge with another on such a level that one knows what they are thinking or feeling. This gift can be used in *animal whispering.* Animal whispering is essentially speaking to animals but it is not as mystical or "woo" as you may originally think. Picture a dolphin for a moment. Dolphins communicate telepathically through a special, supersonic radar. They use certain sound waves and possess the ability to speak to others of their kind through frequencies which are very real and accessible, even though we humans don't or can't attune to them. Now let's look at bats; some bat species use echolocation to essentially "see" in the dark. They use soundwaves formed through echo, which bounce off walls and other physical objects, to help them navigate and see/ sense. So does it truly come as any surprise to both discover and find out that some humans can operate on a level above the norm?

Many autistic people are capable of advanced and extremely evolved gifts in the artistic, mathematical or musical fields... there are real spiritual masters, psychic healers and clairvoyants who are capable of forms of telepathy, extrasensory insight and precognition, and various other enhanced gifts.

Empaths have these abilities. Being connected to such an amplified and evolved level of empathy makes you deeply sensitive to subtle and often spiritual energy. Animals are in tune with this energy, with a world where "seeing" only with two physical eyes or perceiving from a limited, 3- dimensional reality are not the only ways to co-exist. And you as an empath can connect to many animals on a subtle and unseen level.

You are a sensitive soul with a big heart. Choosing a path or career aligned to helping other humans such as the elederly, the disabled or disadvantaged, or some group or organization which needs help, and further being a guide and channel for them, is a route many empaths choose to take. You tend to feel more comfortable around animals or in nature where you can just be yourself, or in any position that makes you act as a channel or conduit for healing and raising humanity's vibration in some way. This is a huge aspect to being an empath- you seek to *raise humanity's vibration* and may find yourself working in the charity, humanitarian or welfare fields. You are genuinely concerned with the welfare and well-being of the earth and all of her inhabitants; and also with consciousness. (Universal consciousness!) As stated with being a musician, artist or creative, you have a gift for tuning in to some higher or morality-based concept, idea or ideal- and this also applies to the paths you may choose to take in environmentalism, charitable or welfare causes and being of service to others through volunteering. There is a lot that could be shared here to but, to keep it short and sweet any hobby, career, path or direction allowing you to make use of your sensitive, caring, empathic and intuitive gifts will enable you to shine!

The Intuitive, Spiritual Healer and Energy Worker

Basically, everything that has been expressed above can be applied here. Even if you do not consider yourself spiritual you are innately spiritually-inclined and perceptive. Being empathic naturally brings an element of spiritual awareness into your daily life and existence, for example you may find yourself when outside in nature or a natural scenery intuitively taking in your surroundings, reflecting on the innate beauty and energetic essence of a space, or allowing your mind to wander in awe-inspiring ways. This is due to you being connected to the subtle- energetic life force present within all living things. This universal life force is also known as chi, ki, Qi or prana- or spirit. It is a state of presence, awareness and centeredness combined with a spiritual and psychic knowing, a "sixth sense" (and seventh and eighth!). Being intrinsically in tune with this means that you see things others don't. You also sense things beyond the five physical senses and may use your natural psychic and spiritual gifts to help others. Many empaths become tarot workers, psychics or clairvoyants, spiritual teachers, healers, shamanic practitioners, sound healers, multi-therapists, or tantric practitioners. You may actually know things without ever having been taught! This is the beauty of your gift and why it should be honored and cherished. Furthermore, this innate ability of yours can greatly assist you in directing your empathic energies towards helpful and purpose-oriented pursuits, as opposed to becoming lost in the negative and ill-intentioned vibes of others (like narcissists, for example).

There is a great saying: *energy goes where awareness*

flows. This applies to you more so than many others. Refer back to the information and perspective in "the artist, creative and visionary" as this can help you understand this aspect of yourself better.

The Independent Worker and 'Self-Employed One'

Finally, because of your inherent dislike of certain characters, roles, interactions and energies- you are most suited to self-employment or highly independent roles. This can manifest in a number of ways such as through being a self-employed plumber, electrician, handywoman or man or owning your own small business. Any "traditional" career or job you choose to go in would best suit you if you were to take on an independent and self-leading role. The main point with this is that you have an aversion and furthermore extreme sensitivity to certain noises which come with 'normal' jobs. Things which most people can tolerate, you feel and experience on a deep level, so much so to the point that specific sounds and frequencies of being can be very harmful to you. Working in an office, for example, can be extremely stressful and even harmful to your empathic nature, as can working in sales or any job where you have to interact with a large number of people on a daily basis. Your extreme sensitivity to harsh noises or toxic environments also means that you don't do well with environmental pollution or harsh chemicals, so any professional path you choose has to have a certain level of self-autonomy. In short, you require sovereignty to choose your tools and channels of work, otherwise certain things can cause severe disruption to your health. Thus, being self-employed equates with shaping your own path and moving to the beat of your own drum, which is paramount as an empath.

Although these are not referring to the different *types* of empath, becoming aware of the varying aspects to the empath personality and your nature allows you to define empathy in its entirety. It can also significantly aid in your journey of discovery and self-development; empathy is an encompassing gift and its applications are vast. Inner and understanding yourself may just be the key to your own personal puzzle, and help to shed light on ambiguities or areas of confusion. It is also important to be aware that not all empaths are the same, just because you resonate with some or all of these elements, it does not mean all other empaths will. To be an empath is to hold a specific blueprint, which may also be seen as the *empath blueprint*, but which paths and channels for self-expression you choose are all up to you.

EMPATH SIGNS

Practical Implications of being the Artist, Creative and Visionary:-

- As a child, you may have found yourself daydreaming and letting your mind wander to unseen worlds and ideas. Your imagination was rich and you may have been bored in social or overly externally stimulating situations, such as parties or social gatherings. You preferred solitude and introspection and always found your mind exploring imaginative realms or abstract ideas.
- You may have naturally had a strong inner knowing that you could come up with better ideas or ingenious solutions to ones being presented in school, or by your teachers and peers. Although never loud nor dominating, your silent inner knowing led to the expansion and development of your hidden gifts and unique creative abilities. People

may have subsequently seen you as the lone wolf or black sheep, or as the shy and quiet one. Yet, inside your skin your mind was working in magical ways!

- Your abstract and creative ways of thinking may not have been appreciated or understood by others. In fact, you may have been bullied, ousted or picked on because of them, simply persecuted for being so unique and original.
- You may have spent a lot of time in your room or in solitude reading, writing, journalism or watching inspirational and educational podcasts or documentaries. Esoteric and metaphysical subjects fascinated you and you had an inner knowing that learning about "strange" or out of the ordinary topics could help with your creativity in some unexplainable way.

Practical Implications of being a Musician, Performer and Storyteller:-

- You found yourself naturally being able to play music, pick up a drum beat or understand aspects relating to advanced

storytelling or performance, without being taught. Reading music may have come easy to you or learning an instrument effortless.
- You had an ability to connect to others on a deep level, even without teaching and could easily and almost effortlessly pick up and adopt many roles. You may have related to characters in plays, performers, or musicians in a deeper way unexplained by your mind, and experienced certain music as a transcendental and 'other-worldly' experience.
- Drama, the Arts and performance-plays interested you strongly, more so than science or math-related subjects. You were advanced in your acting skills and subsequently may have been chosen for leading roles.
- When in a public place or at any traditional societal gathering or event, with music, you often had this unexplainable urge to dance and be completely free; however felt something holding you back, as if you knew you would be judged or appear crazy. Unlike other people dancing, you knew deep down, a feeling in your gut, that you can

change the mood and tone of the room or space simply from your liberated dancing.
- Being the quiet and reserved one in a group was your role growing up, yet there would always be moments where you could feel a big shift in energy and in that moment you would step up. You may have surprised the people around you, even those you know and consider close, and you would suddenly and momentarily take center stage. Some piece of wisdom, perspective, gift or talent would shine through and from this conversation or group activity would change course- usually always in a positive and inspirational or healing direction.

Practical Implications of being a Dreamer, Seer and Psychic:-

- You often had dreams you couldn't explain yet knew were sending you a message or direct insight in some way. Dreams held a strong significant meaning and you knew this even before reading and learning about what was occurring, or before ever being taught.

- You may have naturally had astral experiences or saw "invisible energy" at night time. This is basically you being able to perceive subtle energy, the universal life force existing in space. Many empaths as children can sense spiritual or subtle energy without knowing what it is, further either having unique nightmares or incredible dreams as a result. (I myself am an empath, and I remember seeing thin silver- golden "threads" like cords in the dark, floating around as if I were under the sea. I never knew what it was and told myself not to be afraid, but I could always sense I was surrounded by some magical and unknown presence.)
- Animal whispering may have come naturally to you and you had a deep and extraordinary bond with plants, flowers and nature. You often felt like you existed on a different wavelength altogether and may have felt more connected to animals and flowers or plants than other people, at times.
- If you embody these empath aspects you also have a deep inner feeling regarding people and places. You would 'just know' if

somewhere didn't feel right or a person didn't have good energy. You also would know which way to go and which route was the best when on an adventure, exploration, or nature walk. Your dreams may have been vivid and you may even have found yourself become bolted out of or into your body from sleep.

- Lucid dreaming and astral projection or travel experiences may have come naturally to you, or you most likely will have spoken to some unforgettable characters in dreams which you "knew" were more than just a dream; they felt real.
- Many empaths when young could literally sense, see or feel spiritual beings otherwise known as ghosts. They were never dark or malevolent, but were neutral or benevolent and had a spiritual or peaceful presence. Alternatively, you could see auras and tune in to the energy of a place.

Practical Implications of being a Healer, Counselor and Therapist:-

- You had a unique way of connecting to

others on a deep level and may have found strangers coming up to you to talk, when in your late teens to early 20s. People had an unexplainable pull to you and knew they could open up to you- they will have even bared their soul without any verbal welcome or invitation.

- You may have had a natural affinity and connection with animals and nature and felt most content in their presence, as if you weren't being judged and could be yourself. You also may have been intrinsically drawn to quantum physics, eastern mythology, Buddhist philosophy and meditation books and further had strong inner recognition of the significance of holistic health and alternative medicine. The Healing Arts, holistic and complementary therapies, alternative medicine and spirituality were all passion areas for you.

- You were always the introverted or introspective one of the family and people around you appreciated or recognized you for your empathic, sincere and non- invasive nature. Although still young, adults recognized that you weren't loud or

extrovert and could be turned to for occasional bouts of wisdom, or to be a listening ear.
- You always held particularly high morals and humanitarian principles and were never afraid to speak your truth on these matters. Despite how shy, quiet or reserved you may have usually appeared amongst peers or schoolmates, when it came to group discussions or opportunities to share your perspective you never, ever held back. You may have been one or two out of 30 who were against whale-hunting, for example; or further may have been one in a handful of students who held a specific viewpoint on some environmental or animal rights issues. In short, your empathy and advanced compassion sparked a fearlessness inside of you.

Practical Implications of being a Carer, Social or Support Worker and Companion:-

- Growing up you may have been particularly shy and introspective and perhaps told you were too sensitive, more often than not! This is because you are extremely compassionate and naturally destined to help others in some way; taking on a caring and supporting role even in your youth came naturally to you. As a child and teenager, you may not have understood this and therefore became shy and quiet as a result; however your true self and core essence was never diminished or darkened.

- You also may have had strong feelings of wanting to be a vet or the like when asked what you want to be when you are older. In school when presented with "archetypal choices" (i.e. army person, vet, actor/ actress, doctor, shop manager etc.) you were innately gravitated towards healing or caring professions. (Or something musical, performance- based or creative!)
- You had a particularly strong aversion to violence and became increasingly disturbed when seeing violent or "hateful" acts and scenes on television, or in movies or the like. When witnessing the suffering of others you took on their pain and frequently became what some like to call "overly emotional or sensitive." In fact, adults frequently said you

were too sensitive and never truly understood the way you felt and experienced the world. You felt the pain and suffering of others and had a strong desire to heal and help transcend these pains.
- Something inside you would spark and a part of you always sensed you could be a catalyst for great healing and planetary or global transformation, just through your thoughts, intentions and emotions alone...

Practical Implications of being the Animal Whisperer, Charity Worker and Volunteer:-

- You may have developed a deep and personal relationship with animals which no one knew about. When visiting zoos, animal sanctuaries, wildlife parks or areas you could speak to animals on an inner level and felt an emotional and verging on telepathic/ psychic connection. Animals to you were and are family, they feel, think and experience a huge array of emotions just like we humans, and you recognize this. Your enhanced intuition and instinctual powers may have extended to your connection with animals.

- When coming across a homeless person in the street you had real and sincere compassion for them, to the point where you felt like you had some duty to ease their suffering. This often translated into pain and feeling their trauma or despair. You never hesitated to offer your last coins of change, current beverage or new food item on you, and if you didn't have anything you most likely went into the nearest shop to buy them something! You also now as an adult feel confident to sit with the homeless from time to time, speak to them on a oneness level and connect. You may use your intuitive and healing abilities to simply listen and change an individual's life.
- You may have also felt different from your family in some unexplainable way, which again manifested as being the lone wolf or black sheep. Your sensitive and empathic nature made you stand out from siblings, cousins, friends or those in your peer groups.

Practical Implications of being the Intuitive, Spiritual Healer and Energy Worker:-

- You were deeply drawn to all things mystically esoteric, spiritual and metaphysical from your mid to late teens. You may have been interested in quantum physics, eastern religions and philosophy, crystals, astrology, divination, supernatural abilities, numerology and ancient wisdom. You possessed a deep knowing of all things and could see beyond people's hidden motives, feelings and intentions.
- In adult life, this ability to see beyond the veil of illusion allowed you to tap into your psychic and intuitive powers further, potentially leading you down pathways of training to become a shaman, energy healer or master in some specific lineage and school of thought. You have always known you had a deeper purpose and that your mission in life is to connect to your own soul, so you can help others do the same. Healing ancestral wounds, past trauma and karmic patterns & cycles is essential and a necessity from your perspective. "Soul work"

is an integral part of your philosophy, beliefs and intentions.
- You may have begun meditating at a young age and read spiritual literature or wisdom infused books on the occult, or spiritual/metaphysical topics. Your dreams may have been vast and profound and you may have naturally begun to astral project or travel and lucid dream. All of your senses become heightened and your love for animals and mother earth increased with the more knowledge you acquired.

Practical Implications of being the Independent Worker and Self- Employed One:-

- You had a particular aversion to certain topics in school and perspectives taught as truth were seen as oppressive or dogmatic (one's that conflicted with your empathic knowing and gut feeling). You were not necessarily an outward rebel but you were an inward one, frequently going against the norm either through speech, written works or self- expression. Structure and oppressive ways made you feel limited, you preferred to come up with your own creative solutions and ways of thinking, and following set orders were only respected if they didn't harm the environment or create inequality amongst teachers and students. Even though you were a child or teenager, you still very much had a strong personal integrity and knowledge of natural law and order, fairness and equality. You wouldn't blindly give your respect to a teacher or elder who you felt didn't deserve it.

- Rules and regulations may have seemed oppressive to you and your political views may have been strongly steered towards liberalism, or the green party. There was always an innate desire to break the mould and create your own path, or only support paths of those who were wholly compassionate with pure intentions.
- Any advocation of war, violence, severe injustice, murder, cruelty or harm towards animals, inequality on a global scale and themes like genocide were met with an extreme disliking and subtle pain. Regardless of how "justified" a certain war was or if everyone else agreed a political decision was

valid; if you felt in your heart and gut that it wasn't, it wasn't. Nothing any teacher or textbook said could make you change your mind.
- Even as a teenager or young adult, your integrity and moral values were always steps above the rest.

EMPATH TYPES

Emotional Empaths

Emotional empaths are the most common and well-known types of empaths, and in reality all empaths are emotional empaths. This is due to empathy being the ability to connect with others on an emotional level. Emotional empaths, therefore, can tune in and merge with others, able to feel their emotions as their own. When expressed positively, you can use this as a great gift, being a guiding light and wayshower through advanced and mature levels of emotional wisdom and expression. It also makes you incredibly susceptible to psychic and subtle influences and abilities, such as all forms of extrasensory perception and telepathy, precognition and the capacity for evolved levels of "mind reading." If, however, you have not yet learned how to stay centered and grounded and further protect yourself from potentially harmful influences, this can have some seriously detrimental effects. You can absorb other people's moods and emotions to the point of being sad, confused, hurt, depressed, or in pain, and often you won't even know why. In this sense you act as an *emotional sponge* and take on every feeling, thought, emotion and impression which accompanies as your own. When mastered, of course, this emotional sensitivity can be used as a gift, and can also be used to get to the bottom of deceitful or ill-intentioned people. You can sense their hidden motives and get to the core of what they are hiding or how they are being untruthful and manipulative.

Intellectual Empaths

Because we naturally associate empathy with emotions and intuition, intellectual empaths are not usually considered as a type of empath. Intellectual empaths, however, possess a unique gift in that they are able to speak and communicate in a rare way. You can merge with another's mind or energy body and come up with information, wisdom, words and phrases which are not known to your conscious mind. For example, if you are an intellectual empath, you may have once read something in a book or heard a piece of information which then became stored in the subconscious. When you next interact with someone some subtle energy triggers your mind into knowing about some seriously complex topics! *Mirroring* behavior, intellect, and mind comes naturally, therefore, and often leaves you with an inner knowing and shock simultaneously, along with the lines of "how did I know this," or "wow- I'm a genius!" You can further adapt your vocabulary, speech, and style to different people from all sorts of backgrounds. So when communicating or interacting with others, you may just change roles or personas and start speaking of unusual, specialist or expanded subject areas. You can essentially adapt to any character due to your highly adaptable and flexible nature.

Intuitive Empaths

If you are an intuitive empath you embody an element of all the different types of empaths. Intuition is a gift which defines the personality and nature of an empath, as intuition is the ability to be in tune with your senses. When you "intuit something" you feel or sense what is about to happen, so when you are connected to your intuition you are connected to your place of knowing and power. You may receive direct wisdom or guidance from your higher self (the higher mind connected to cosmic and universal consciousness, and the divine), or just know which route to take or decision to make. Being intuitive, therefore, leads to all the other unique aspects and types of empathy. This advanced intuition can be used as a gift, such as in healing, psychic or spiritual phenomena, helping others or animals, or through counseling and caring or support roles.

Ultimately all empaths are intuitive, but if you resonate strongly with this one then you are connected to your intuitive mind above all else. Your intuition is your guiding light and the basis for all of your choices and empathic gifts.

Psychic or Medical Empaths

Psychic or medical empaths take on the physical ailments of others. Like an emotional empath who absorbs the emotions of others, psychic or medical empaths pick up on the physical state and energy of other people's bodies. This can present itself in many ways such as through physically taking on the symptoms, aches, and pains of another; for example feeling like you have a pain in your leg when someone else has a pain in their leg, or briefly getting headache symptoms when near someone with a headache. Or by sensing the energetic and physical state of another- you may *just know* that someone has a stomach ache or is going through a painful moon cycle (period), or perhaps is dealing with a toothache. (The applications are vast!) This is because you are connected to many dimensions including the subtle and spiritual therefore you sense things above and beyond the norm. Blockages, ailments, distortions and imbalances can be seen and sensed, to an extent- and this is done through extrasensory perception combined with a strong and powerful intuition.

Many psychic empaths also go on to become healers or therapists due to this special gift including physicians, massage therapists, shamanic practitioners, reflexologists, aromatherapists, shiatsu practitioners, energy workers or bodyworkers. Some empaths can even *see* energy blockages directly in another, experienced through a combination of color and feeling the distortion or issue through sight.

Spiritual Empaths

Spiritual empaths are essentially the natural mediums, psychics, clairvoyants, and "channels." You can act as a channel for many things and aspects of consciousness and higher awareness to shine through, such as by connecting to the spirit or some 'subtle-energetic' thought form. If you are a spiritual empath, you have the ability to not only communicate with the spirit or some higher power but to also *feel* the emotional, mental and physical (medical) state of another person, animal or natural entity. You are like emotional and psychic/medical empaths, but with a more holistic and encompassing understanding. Many spiritual empaths go on to become great healers, spiritual teachers or guides as you can, literally, tune in and connect to any body, dimension, frequency or subtle state of existence. There is always some genuine desire to do good and be of service and never to harm or exert an unhealthy and boastful ego. You may also be clairvoyant, clairsentient, and clairaudient, therefore, sense, feel and hear things from other dimensions.

Animal Empaths

As an animal empath, you possess the unique gift to communicate and connect with animals on a deep and rare level. This can be expressed through animal whispering as mentioned earlier or you may evolve this gift into simply becoming more mindful and present with it. Many animal empaths feel more connected and comfortable around the presence of animals (as opposed to being around humans), and animals sense this. There is an underlying feeling of 'magic' when connected to an animal, such as a horse, dog or cat, in an empathic way, and the animals too sense the intentions and awareness of the empath. Even if you do not necessarily consider yourself an animal communicator or whisperer connecting to this aspect of yourself can enhance your life greatly, and increase your confidence in your abilities simultaneously.

Plant Empaths

You are intrinsically connected to the plants, trees, flowers, and natural entities of the world. Like an emotional empath who can tune into others' emotions, you have a unique ability to connect to plants on a deep level. You have a natural intuition about what plants and flowers need and may not have ever read a specialist book on how to grow, care or maintain special plants. Simultaneously you may find that seeds and flowers grow and thrive in your presence. This is due to your *aura* and the intentions you subtly exhibit. Plants, like people and animals, respond to energy and subtle impressions, and many plant empaths make great shamans and healers due to the ability to feel the spirit on the plant queen and kingdoms.

If you are a plant empath you may walk into a friend or family member's home and instantly know that the plant may need fresh water or may be wanting to be moved to a different location. Furthermore, you can actually receive guidance from trees and flowers and communicate on a telepathic level!

Environmental Empaths

As an environmental empath, you have a fine-tuned sense to the natural wonders of the earth. You can sense and 'read' physical locations, natural objects, and places of energetic significance. Sacred sites have a special resonance to you and you may be able to feel things beyond the physical senses from stepping into a place, for example, a holy site, a temple on sacred grounds, or places like Stonehenge. Environmental empaths are also known as *geometric* empaths due to the geographical element of their gifts. Natural objects such as gemstones, crystals, and rocks can be connected with to receive information, and you can sense and feel other people's emotions, memories, and experiences when stepping into a place.

When honed and developed environmental empaths can use their abilities like a compass, tuning into the physical and environmental locations for all sorts of extrasensory experiences and wisdom to come through. It is also important as an environmental empath to spend time in nature as you often need to 'recharge' due to your heightened sensitivity to external influence.

Introverted Empaths

Introverted empaths are the type of empaths many people mistake the empath personality for. Being an empath is not synergistic with being introverted, however, they are linked. Introverts are people who feel more comfortable in the inner worlds of being and subsequently enjoy activities like reading, journaling, introspection, gaming, gardening, and solitude over any extroverted or loud activities and interactions. As empaths generally prefer one to one or more intimate, authentic, and real conversation and connection, if you resonate with this type of empath personality then you display the qualities of an introvert. You do not necessarily inherently dislike social situations and are not 'not extrovert,' however, you do have an aversion of some sort to overly loud and domineering characters and busy social scenarios.

As an introverted empath, you can use your love of solitude, one-to-one or smaller interactions and introspective activities to develop your empathic nature and gifts further.

Activist Empaths

Activist empaths can also be called 'the warrior-empath.' This is because, quite simply, you are a warrior and an activist and stand up for what you believe in. You use your empathic gifts and unique perceptive insight and intuition to help others in some way whether that be an activist for animals, other people, or the environment. Activist empaths have a sense of mission or purpose and are always strong, bold, courageous, and fearless, therefore making compassionate and powerful leaders. You still take time to recharge and connect to your inner source of power, but you are also strong in your beliefs and convictions and harness your empathy to do good in the world.

Many activist empaths go on to become campaigners, politicians, leaders, or speakers or may choose to channel their abilities in some creative or artistic field with a big vision.

As you can see from the descriptions there are many types of empaths. They all fundamentally share the same unique quality which allows for your unique insight and perception. This gift is *intuition*.

2

TWO SIDES OF AN EMPATH'S COIN

EMPATH MYTHS AND MISCONCEPTIONS

1. Empaths are over- sensitive, weak and melodramatic.

One of the greatest misconceptions to being an empath is that you are weak. Confusing your sensitivity for anything but a superpower is a mistake, and unfortunately too many people make this mistake. It is this misconception and myth which leads to a lot of the abuse inflicted upon we empaths; we suffer at the hands of narcissists and other toxic characters who we frequently attract into our orbits, simply because they misperceive us to be weak and feel they can use and abuse us. Being labelled spineless, melodramatic or feeble may be common, as can being hypersensitive. But being sensitive is a beautiful gift and empaths are far from weak! In fact, it is we empaths who are the strongest type of people on this earth, and it is something which should be honored. As an empath, you are known for your heightened state of emotions and developed ability to connect to the thoughts and inner feelings of others. You can sense on so many levels, and for people who are less receptive and connected to their inner essence this can be greatly misperceived.

The truth is, many people are extroverted and rely heavily on external distractions, connections, social events or scenarios and entertainment. You, on the other hand, are very comfortable and content in the realm of emotions and simply "being." This brings us onto the next myth.

2. Empaths are shy and anti-social

You are far from shy or anti-social, but many people perceive you as these things. This is because you are happy to function on a chilled and relaxed and often non-verbal level. Conversation which stimulates you in some way is favored and if there is no depth or passionate and interesting discussion, you may choose to remain silent in a social setting, further being an observer and taking everything in. It is this silence and contentedness which some mistake for shyness. Yet, you are highly perceptive and can feel high, happy or energized from observing and connecting to others on a subtle level. You don't like gossip, pointless chat or excessive communication just for the sake of communication, so people see you as anti-social. Expanding on from what was briefly mentioned in the last myth and misconception, many people are extroverted whereas you are introvertedly inclined. If not an introvert, you most certainly like reflecting and turning towards introspection. It is in introspection where you can connect to your essence, subtle energy and an emotional depth- and you thrive in these places! But this can be misperceived.

3. Empaths are self- centered and self- absorbed.

In apparent contradiction to the last myth and misconception is the fact that some choose to see you as self- absorbed and even selfish; this couldn't be further from the truth. You are incredibly selfless, which is the opposite of selfishness. So why do some misperceive you as selfish and self- centered? The most simple and all-encompassing answer is that many people don't get you. They live in a world of non-empathy as a basic foundational character. They are still overcome with tendencies of narcissism, selfishness, egotistical energy and action, and separation-based thoughts and emotions; they don't operate or exist on the same frequency as you. Now, this is not advocating that you are superior or "better than" them, but, on a level it needs to be recognized that your core programming is functioned to a different vibration and frequency. The real world practical implications of this are that your empathy and deep care is mistaken for self-centeredness. Just like the analogy used at the beginning of this chapter regarding walking into a room and you "tuning in" to a certain frequency, many people don't see you. They don't see or understand you at all, in truth. Some of your most beautiful qualities including unconditional love and compassion, deep care and consideration for others, a healing and supportive nature, and, of course, empathy in its optimum; are misperceived. They may not even be received by some due to the shield some of us wear.

A prime representation of this myth is the following. You are sat in a room silent, introspective and empathically connected. You have entered into a social gathering or situation with intentions of deep and authentic connection, being the friend in need or consciously opening yourself up to be ready to give advice, love, care and support. Referring to the empath qualities expressed earlier, you naturally take on the role of a caregiver, counsellor or healer/therapist. Now, this is your vibration- it is you in your realest without any mask or facade. Yet, to loud, narcissistic, emotionally closed off, extroverted or overly masculine and aggressive characters (perhaps not all simultaneously, but any one applies) you are appearing self-centered. Quite simply, you don't exist on their frequency therefore they can't see you. They have put up a shield to your truth and empathy because they have most likely closed off this part of themselves, or at the very least not consciously worked to integrate it into their core programming and personality. *You operate on different frequencies.* Another example is that you shine in the most selfless and unconditionally giving way possible to mankind, yet people see you as selfish or manipulative. They can't understand that you truly are a giving, kind and authentically love-fuelled character, so your actions and motivations *must be* selfish, or you *must* have a hidden agenda. This "must" is, of course, their own ego illusions and projections; their own distorted beliefs and patterns of thinking.

4. Empaths are lazy and lack drive, ambition or passion.

The perception that empaths are lazy and further lack drive or ambition is yet another distortion of the non-empathic mind. Empathy as explored is a gift often derived from the silence and the space. The "silence and the space" is the emptiness of being that is also the source of creation. Through introspection, conscious moments of introversion (not relying on external stimuli or constant entertainment!), creative, artistic and imaginative self-expression, and getting in tune with your listening and natural counselling skills, which are all intrinsic to the empath personality, you become absorbed into a different reality altogether. It is from this space where *incredible* ideas, thoughts and catalysts into action occur. Again, a lot of extroverted people believe or misperceive genius and innovation to come from the only thing they know, action, noise and busyness, sound and movement. But, are sound and movement not met equally with silence and space? This is the key to understanding yourself and coming to terms with this misconception of others.

From a different perspective, the truth is, many of us empaths do suffer from moments of laziness, but this is purely due to the fact that we are taking on so much from others. We may become temporarily lost in a reality of literally becoming a caregiver, counsellor or therapist to those we love, and this in itself leaves us neglecting other areas of our lives and more importantly; personal ambitions. It may lead you to become an emotional dumping ground or taking on so much external baggage that you always feel tired, hence the lack of passion and drive.

5. Empaths are moody as hell

Oh dear. Would it be too judgemental to call this ignorant as hell?! Being perceived as moody is, in fact, a sincere level of ignorance. It is ignore-ance, the decision to ignore something and tune it out of one's reality. And this is what some people do to your compassion, empathy and desire to help, heal or hold space. The truth is that many empaths focus more on others than themselves and this can leave them open to actual mood swings, because they (you) take on the problems of others, or leave you open to not being moody but going into deep introspection. This tendency towards withdrawal and introspection is not because you are self-absorbed or immersed in your own feelings and thoughts, it is because you are either unconsciously or consciously absorbing everyone else's sh*t. You intuitively and instinctively feel the feelings of others and this involves their worries, concerns, pain and struggles. It also, however, involves their *illusions*, judgements, distortions and harmful and ill-intended, or not so pure and holy, wishes and mental projections towards you or those you love. In short, taking on so much can be very harmful to yourself, and one result of this is to become "down." But you may not actually be down, you may just be transmuting it all by going into a contemplative and transmutive space. A lot of the time you don't realize you do it, so why is it that you should 1- be moody or not upbeat and joyous (introspective) as a result of other people's illusions and issues, and then 2- be persecuted or judged for it?!

The answer is you shouldn't. Learning how to center yourself and put up strong and healthy boundaries is a key part of the empath journey, and further essential to your survival.

6. Empaths are mentally ill, crazy or have serious psychological problems.

Chronic Fatigue Syndrome, insomnia, headaches, nervous tension and other physical and mental health issues and ailments can arise in empaths, and it is important to be aware of this and follow the steps necessary to protect, love and heal yourself. This is due to being a magnet to others' energies and issues, further having unprotected boundaries. But, a whole, healed and balanced empath is *not* crazy, nor do they suffer from mental health or psychological issues. In some cases, empaths can become depressed and suffer from the effects of taking on too much and being an emotional baggage dumping ground, yet this is rare and perhaps only happens once in a lifetime,until the empath finds themselves and learns about their true nature. Being polluted by other people's harmful energy is not something which should make you be seen as having a mental health problem, for the root of the problem is not with you as the empath but with the people doing the projecting and twisting. Any pattern of thinking, belief or perception that is not true and essentially self-created, faulty and distorted, is a distortion. Because empathy is primarily an emotional gift and quality, your perceived problems may stem from emotional manipulation of others or through the very same love and care or compassion you project.

Remember, just because you hold certain intentions and motivations in life it doesn't mean everything else does. Being an empath is a very unique and often intense, or at least emotionally charged, persona and lifetime experience to take on. You may also take on a significant amount of *karma*, and this is a reality which can lead to considerable healing, compassion and the strengthening of gifts when honed and harnessed.

EMPATH STRENGTHS

Here we explore the main strengths of being an empath.

1. Easygoing and relaxed nature

Despite what many people may initially think of you, you are extremely easy going with a relaxed nature and calm demeanour. You handle stress well and often thrive in situations many would get nervous, chaotic or even frantic. Things which may be overwhelming to others can be handled with ease due to your empathic nature. The same is true to embarrassing situations and experiences that cause major confusion or ambiguity- you merge with it all and use your evolved intuition, compassion and empathy to navigate tricky waters.

2. Adaptability and openness to change

You are so adaptable and flexible that it is no wonder many *Pisces* are empaths. Pisces are the 12th star sign of the zodiac and are considered the *old souls* of the zodiac. They are also seen by many as synonymous with empaths, so learning about the strengths and qualities of the Pisces star sign can help you to better understand your own empathic gifts. In short, you are easy to adapt and go with the flow with not much in life fazing you. This is a rare gift!

3. Genius mindset and amazing imagination

Possibly two of your greatest gifts are your genius mentality and ability to connect to advanced and evolved levels of imaginative thought and expression. Everything that has been shared in chapter 1 applies here, so re- read that section for clarification. (*The Artist, Creative and Visionary,* and *The Musician, Performer and Storyteller* sections.)

4. Compassion, acceptance and understanding

"The Healer, Counsellor and Therapist"and "The Carer, Social or Support Worker, and Companion" in chapter 1 can be revisited.

5. Listening and problem- solving skills

Your listening and natural counselling skills have

been stated quite a few times now, but what also needs to be stressed is your problem-solving skills. You have a unique ability to see things a certain way and, combined with your imagination and advanced creativity, this can lead to highly significant victories and accomplishments in the innovative, intellectual and cognitive realms. It may be easy to assume that empaths are just emotional creatures with sensitive and spiritual or compassionate natures, but there is an incredible intellectual and analytical side to you. Your empathy extends to the ability to "read minds," and this manifests into the cognitive, problem-solving and mental reasoning aspects of life.

6. Purity of mind, heart and soul...

Being an empath means you have one of the purest hearts, minds and souls. Your purity is birthed from your advanced emotional frequency; simply put, you operate at a much higher consciousness and evolved state of feeling, perception and being.You are connected to your soul and even if you are the type of empath who does not consider themselves spiritual, you are deeply in tune with the beauty of life, nature and the universe. You perceive subtle energy and are connected to the subconscious realms in a unique and profound way.

7. Chameleon-like

You are a bit of a chameleon, dear empath, and this is a wonderful trait to possess. Your personal strength, knowing and self-assurity comes from your advanced intuition and ability to *know thyself*; you are deeply compassionate, perceptive and understanding and this makes you highly adaptable. It also makes you incredibly fluid, like water, with a "go with the flow" nature and aspect to your personality and character.

8. Human lie detectors

Being a human lie detector is a pretty heavy responsibility, for you can literally see beyond the surface and behind the veil of illusion. Peoples' ill-intentions, untrue motivations and hidden agendas can all be felt by you, just like a snake senses subtle energy through their tongues and through the ground. But being so perceptive and intuitive does not have to be heavy, when you are balanced, whole and centered with strong boundaries it can be a blessing. You can use this gift to help others, such as through being a counsellor or support worker, or through taking on a diplomatic and mediating role. This gift can also help you navigate life's waters and fires with ease, integrity and grace.

EMPATH STRUGGLES

1. Over or hypersensitive

Being so sensitive can be a recurring theme and issue in your life, especially in moments of weakness or vulnerability, or when you struggle from low or weak boundaries. In normal cases, your sensitivity is a superpower- not a weakness or setback. But when you lose touch with your essence and your true self, or simply decrease your boundaries you are prone to being oversensitive or hypersensitive. This is because you are an *emotional sponge* and sometimes an emotional dumping ground for other people's baggage and bs! It is a sad truth, but this is the reality of being an empath. Before you have learned to ground yourself and protect your energies you become super sensitive to all the various currents and impressions swimming around. You may unconsciously pick up on EVERYONE'S problems and internal struggles, and this may even extend to the not so helpful or loving thoughts and opinions of others. The result? You have severe difficulty in living your life with peace, bliss and balance and also in staying connected to your empathic gifts & strengths. The other result is that this leaves you feeling *emotionally and mentally drained*.

2. Emotionally and mentally drained

Due to everything mentioned in the last point one of your main struggles in life is becoming emotionally drained. You are prone to absorbing all of the external feelings, currents and energies around you and due to your genuinely helpful nature you often open yourself up to this reality, intentionally. But it takes quite a few times throughout life to realize and finally integrate the lesson and teaching- the lesson that not everyone is as pure, honest or kind-hearted and sincere as you. This makes you open to energy vampires, toxic characters and narcissistic personalities. Selfish and abusive people (one can be mentally and emotionally abusive) see your kind and giving, and often gentle and compassionate, nature and seek to take, take and take! They get attracted to your heart and inner light like moths to a flame. This leaves you incredibly depleted. You may become depleted of your empathy, time, sincerity, inner fire and light, resources, money or love and affection, or in extreme cases you may actually be conned. Fortunately, by educating yourself on your strengths and seeking to integrate and embody them fully, you can put up a healthy and strong shield against all of this, and further overcome your lifelong empath struggles.

3. Prone to energy vampires and narcissists

This point is so significant that it needs a section of its own. Possibly the most fundamental lesson you will learn in this lifetime is that of the empath-narcissist dynamic. Narcissists are selfish, highly manipulative, self-centered and egotistical. They gravitate towards people like empaths because they see kindness, heart and empathy as a *weakness*, not a strength or beautiful gift which should be honored and cherished. At first, narcissists appear charming, intelligent, warm and affectionate, they can manipulate you into believing they are your best friend or ideal partner, but this is just a facade. There is always some hidden motive or ill-intention deep down. A narcissist can be a "general" narcissist or they can be extreme. We explore this more in later chapters, but, for now, the main point to be aware of is that narcissists don't care about you; they don't care about your feelings, love, good intentions or supreme and unconditional generosity or compassion. Just as giving is a part of your core programming, taking and abusing is part of theirs. The real life implications of this is that once you have encountered a narcissist and entered into a bond or relationship with them, whether that be consciously or unconsciously, it can be very hard to heal and healing and recovery may take a long time. It can also leave you feeling confused and questioning your own intentions and self-worth. Narcissists are master manipulators.

As for energy vampires, they will drain you of everything you have. Other toxic characters include compulsive liars, abusers, persecutors and psychopaths or sociopaths. Extreme narcissism is a case of the latter two.

4. Too kind and giving

Your strength is that you are genuine, kind, selfless and giving. Your weakness and therefore struggle is that you can be too much of these things, you don't know when to cut off or put up healthy and essential boundaries. Many empaths don't learn this lesson until later in life, such as mid to late twenties or early thirties. Adolescence, the teenage years and young adulthood can be particularly tricky as an empath, as these periods of life find you asking questions such as; "how can the world be such a cold place?" "How could s/he do that to me, I truly trusted them!" And, "This is too much to bear...why do feel I everyone's shadow, pain and suffering so strongly?!" An intrinsic effect of your kindness, even when young, is the natural capacity you hold for taking on other people's illusions and despair. Just seeing a simple act of violence on t.v. or in a film can leave you feeling heartbroken, wholly depleted and low. Your kindness and heart combined with often unbreakable compassion signifies that the world's darkness and suffering is too much for your soft and gentle heart. We expand on this in chapter 4.

3

ARE YOU AN EMPATH OR JUST BEING EMPATHIC?

ORDINARY EMPATHY VS BEING AN EMPATH

*E*mpathy is a gift, as established, and being an empath is *integrating, embodying* and *balancing* empathy into daily life, into your perpetual character and persona. You may be thinking, "why is it useful to know this, to know the difference between being an empath and possessing or exhibiting empathy?" It is important to be aware of the difference so that you can navigate life and yourself with ease and understanding. Knowing when you are fully connected to your empath self, assuming you are one, or when you are simply displaying empathy as a non-empath allows you to know yourself, your intentions and your responses better. It is like being a doctor with a vast array of specialist knowledge or simply being fascinated in healing and science, and sharing your self- acquired wisdom from time to time. It is also like being a musician, who lives, breathes and practices/plays music daily, or someone who likes to occasionally pick up an instrument or sing. You can be knowledgeable, insightful and skilled in medicine or music without being a doctor or musician respectively. The same is true for being an empath or possessing the capacity for empathy.

* * *

Empathy: is the ability to tune in and connect to other people's feelings. An empathic person is capable of deep and authentic emotional connection, compassion and understanding, but does not necessarily identify with merging with this character trait as part of their core and fundamental identity. An empathic person can be moved and brought to intense feelings and heart-felt responses or impressions.

An empath: is someone who takes on the feelings,

thoughts and impressions of others to the extent that they literally become one with those feelings. It is as if they are directly, actively and consciously experiencing those feelings themselves.

* * *

If you are an empath, you not only feel for others but also absorb the feelings of others. Your emotional awareness, wisdom and intelligence exist on a much higher level and frequency. You can pick up on unspoken beliefs and opinions as well, and very much act in the same way as some animals. The saying that snakes can sense human fear and subsequently act or respond based on your feelings and intentions towards them, works very much in the same way as a true empath. Snakes pick up on energy through the ground and sense through a special sensory organ on the roof of their mouths. Well, an empath absorbs and picks up on the *overall vibration* of another. The key to be aware of is that our thoughts, opinions, beliefs, intentions, self-talk, mindset, emotions, feelings and virtually all impressions construct our holistic vibe and frequency. If someone's overall frequency is giving off bad or ill-intentioned energy, you pick up on this. If someone is in need of healing, advice or compassionate assistance, you equally pick up on this. In essence you respond to people's energies and intentions towards both yourself and others.

THE SUBTLE ENERGY BODY/FIELD: BEING AWARE OF THE AURA

We all have an electromagnetic energy field also known as the aura. Science defines this very real circle of energy surrounding all living and conscious organisms as an electromagnetic field, or energy field, and those spiritually aware define it as an aura. In truth, they are both one and the same as they both describe the "bubble" of energy circulating the human body and other living organisms. Aura stems from the Greek word for *breeze*, and this can be seen to portray the human aura in its essence. Essentially, our auras are a combination of electric, magnetic and spiritual-subtle energy wherein all of our thoughts, beliefs, emotions and subtle impressions navigate and pass through. We emit certain frequencies or codings of information and sensory data, through the impulses in our brain and body. These in turn are transmitted through the aura extending just above and beyond the physical body. This is how emotions can be felt without words being used to describe them, or how some people can sense things psychically, telepathically or clairvoyantly. The aura can ultimately be seen as a transmitter and receiver of consciousness and all thoughts, emotions and subtle sensations.

There has never been much scientific proof of the presence of the aura, despite the thousands to millions of first hand and real-life experiences of those who attuned to subtle and spiritual energy! But in recent years the emergence of *Kirlian photography* has provided some fascinating evidence supporting the existence of the aura. What is even more fascinating, however, is that empaths *actively engage and work with their aura every day*. In other words, you are so in tune with your subtle energy bodies and the subconscious inner workings, that you don't even need the proof or scientific words to describe what naturally occurs. You sense things, see things and pick up on things beyond the five physical senses. You can feel out unspoken feelings and thoughts or know if someone is happy, sad, anxious, excited, scared, or the like. You also go a step further- and this is why and how many empaths are seen as psychic, or in possession of spiritual gifts- by sensing actual physical ailments. You may walk into a room and know if someone is sick, ill or in pain, or suss out the specific organ or bodily area which is causing grievance.

The ability to do such things is achieved through your aura, the electromagnetic bubble of energy surrounding you and everyone else. Because you are attuned to a personal frequency of helping, healing and using compassionate understanding and insight to be of service to others, you receive emissions unlike others. Other people's energy bodies are constantly interacting with your own so that you can choose to help and be of assistance in some way. Subtle vibrations and intentions are sent and you pick up on them. It is like having a radio attuned to a specific frequency… this is the most accurate and understandable way to visualize the essence of being an empath. Now, in terms of real-world implications this means that if you haven't yet learned how to put up healthy and strong boundaries, you will still be prone to negative energy and acting as a sort of sponge for emotional and psychic baggage. You can also, of course, be prone to absorbing negative or harmful energy, or feeling low and unwell without cause. The other end of the spectrum is that once you have strong and healthy boundaries, your whole vibration becomes one of mindful and conscious extrasensory perception, psychic ability and subtle-sensitivities; sensitivities which allow you to help others and act as a catalyst for other people's healing and transformation, instead of picking up on all the negative and BS! There are two sides to the coin, so hopefully the wisdom and guidance in this book will allow you to embody the latter.

A lot of this is already covered in detail throughout these chapters, therefore, for now, let's briefly look at how you can do this.

- Determine your own emotions, beliefs and feelings. Create healthy boundaries and put up a shield so that you can distinguish what is yours, and what isn't.
- Find joy and pleasure in your gifts and empathic abilities. Listening to your body and your senses enables you to *enjoy being an empath* which in turn creates more of the positive and beneficial experiences and associations.
- Focus on kindness, compassion and sincerity. These, amongst your giving and selfless nature, are your main strengths.
- Develop your connection to animals and nature. The natural world and various forms

of "animal whispering" can serve as great inspiration for empathy and also keep you connected to your true self.
- Your higher self- find ways to strengthen it. Intrinsically linked with being an empath is the connection you have with your higher self, the evolved and higher functioning aspect of mind, heart, soul and holistic self. There are many ways to strengthen and fully integrate your higher self into daily life!
- Stay clear of the illusions, negativity and myths. All of the empath misconceptions and myths should be learned about, but once you are knowledgeable you should steer clear of falling into other people's illusions and ignorance. Negativity serves no one- let alone yourself.
- Be aware of toxic personalities and narcissistic characters… set boundaries, practice self- care and self- love, and protect yourself from narcissists and toxic people. This is essential!
- Try to transcend being appeasing, people- pleasing and severely codependent. Because of your natural affinity for emotional connection and intimacy (whether platonic

or not), you may unconsciously steer towards codependence and other unhealthy habits. Meditation and light forms of self-therapy such as sound therapy can really help.
- Surround yourself with other like-minded people. Empaths are great company for you, and so are organizations or groups committed to helping others, the environment or those less fortunate in some way. Interact with the kindred spirits and sensitive but strong souls of the world; they are the ones who will help you thrive.

THE ROLE OF THE EXTERNAL TRIGGER

The main difference between possessing empathy and being an empath lies in the role of the external trigger. For empaths, we do not need an external trigger- our thoughts, motivations and inner desires are already attuned to an empathically caring and compassionate way of being and feeling. Our reality is aligned with being an empath and therefore responding to people and situations in a completely empathic way. To a non-empath, however, feeling real and sincere empathy requires an external trigger; an action or experience to inspire them to empathy. Understanding this crucial difference and further being aware of the types of experiences and situations that spark empathy in non-empaths can enhance and expand your understanding of your own empath nature. Below we explore some of the key situations and interactions which may arise to initiate authentic empathy.

1. Extreme acts of violence, aggression or "evil"

Wrongdoings, pain and harm caused to others, violence and serious aggression, and moments of "evil" are all catalysts to empathy. Darkness often provides space and opportunity for others to see the light, and this is exactly what occurs in both non-empaths and within yourself. Acts of violence or extreme darkness and despair on t.v, in films or through the news can be particularly catalytic, as can witnessing any first hand. Observing such scenes whether through a screen or in the flesh creates a new portal for empathic feelings and communication, hence acting as an external trigger.

2. The pain and suffering of others

Any and all experiences with pain and suffering is a major trigger for empathy. Empathy is defined by the ability to feel and experience another's feelings, so being witness to their pain and suffering is the ultimate spark to and for empathy. Assuming you are an empath, you don't necessarily need to see a particularly extreme or vivid scenario of despair, struggle or trauma for your empathy to be sparked. It comes naturally to you. However, for a non-empath these things are extremely powerful. Pain pulls on their heart strings, it sends a ripple throughout their body which basically says *I feel for you, I am one with you, I understand and emphasize.* It is only narcissists who are truly incapable of experiencing such empathy and inner sensations.

3. Injustice, minor or major

Injustice is another trigger and this can be minor or major. Seeing injustice either to others, animals or the environment and sustaining planet we reside in also acts as a spark and catalyst to those deep and honest feelings of empathy we are all capable of experiencing. Injustice for the empath is ingrained and integrated into one's personality and core programming- any sign of injustice to another automatically and instantaneously gets an empath's attention and compassion. But, for someone who does not consider themselves an empath, being witness to severe injustices is a worthy external trigger. Injustice comes in many forms, shapes and sizes and may include seeing someone majorly wronged financially or practically, someone abused or treated with violence and aggression, someone misusing a position of power or authority, or issues of moral and/or spiritual injustice.

4. Being trusted with personal stories and deep moments of sharing

When someone opens up and bares their heart or soul, this can often inspire deep and sincere feelings of empathy. There is a certain level of trust given when a stranger or friend and loved one in need opens up to you; it is as if they are silently but very apparently saying "I trust you with my deepest feelings and concerns, thank you for your empathy." In fact, in moments like these the story-teller is ultimately providing the listener with an opportunity for growth and self-development, and, again, it would take a real narcissist to not be able to feel and experience empathy in such situations.

4

THE EMPATH'S OWN PROBLEMS AND STRUGGLES

THE MISUNDERSTOOD BEHAVIORS

We have covered quite a significant amount in empath myths and misconceptions, so in this section let's target a few specific behaviors and get to the root of both the true empath nature and how others perceive you.

Holding Space: Detaching and becoming seemingly "aloof"

To hold space is to muster up all of your might and become strong, centered and aligned for someone else's journey and path. Many empaths do this, and frequently, and you may not even know you are doing it. It is in your nature to tune in to the pain, despair, suffering or problems of others and seek to help heal them. Well, you do this through becoming a sort of conduit, or channel, for healing and light to shine through. Through your empathy, capacity for great compassion and the love and healing thoughts you send them, you can essentially hold space- and it is from space where everything arises. Creation is space, it comes from space and permeates in and around it; creation doesn't just disappear or cease to exist. We humans are natural channels and energy conduits for thoughts, feelings, emotions, beliefs, epic epiphanies and spiritual awareness to shine through. But we don't all consciously or mindfully open ourselves up to this reality. As an empath, you do your thoughts and inner motivations alone create a unique vibration within which essentially tells the world; "I am here for you. I am love, I am compassion and I am non-judgemental awareness. I am happy to listen to you and devote my time and energy into being of assistance." It's a powerful and extraordinary gift to possess.

Unfortunately, not everyone understands this and for those few people who are actively against healing and self-development, they can misconstrue your intentions and personal energy altogether. The key word here is projection, they *project* their own insecurities and ignorance onto you. Some people may consciously do this, such as energy vampires, narcissists or other toxic characters, but for others its less conscious and apparent. The best analogy to use here is in relation to sound wave frequencies and natural phenomena. Dogs and many other animals can hear parts of the sound spectrum we humans can't, but it doesn't mean that these specific frequency and high or low pitched sounds don't exist! Henceforth, you appear aloof, detached or disconnected from your physical environment; when in reality you are more connected than most.

Needing your alone time and solitude: Not wanting to connect or be sociable

The appearance of being unfriendly, cold, distant or extremely unsociable can all be assumed and seen when in fact you just need your alone time. Unlike non-empaths, you need to recharge your batteries. If you don't spend sufficient time in introspection, rest and rejuvenation or self-healing you can become very disoriented and drained. Other people's feelings, emotions and welfare continuously take up your time and despite how others may misperceive you, you are incredibly selfless and generous with your time and energy. It is because of this fact alone that you require so much time in solitude and rest. Furthermore, you *thrive* on connection; connection forms the basis and foundation of your whole existence. One of the main empath fears is disconnection, or separation. The way you think, feel and perceive is very different to how others experience their reality, so your truth may not be understood or even seen. Sometimes it is only when you take on a highly verbal or extroverted role and persona that people become aware of your true motivations and feelings, before this they may have been completely none the wiser regarding your innate empathic nature and daily reality. Just because *you* know what you go through, it does not mean others do!

Thus, needing your solitude to recharge so you can be your brilliant and beautiful, caring and compassionate self infused with wisdom and strength, solely for others, will often be seen as you being disconnected and anti-social. This can fortunatly be overcome through learning to speak up and be more expressive, further not feeling ashamed or selfish in speaking your truth and defending yourself. Many times in life you will need to call the moon the moon, even when you think everyone else is already aware of it...

Embodying the *empath blueprint*: Appearing moody

Human life is prone to illusion. In fact, we can all be seen to be existing under the veil of illusion, as life itself is both a multidimensional and mystical experience. The empath blueprint is your ultimate energetic blueprint, you at your best and highest frequency self. When you are in this space and connected to your true self, you can appear deeply moody or down. This may not be a problem if it wasn't for the fact that people treat you in a certain way because of it. Being seen as moody when you are in fact in high spirits and in a beautiful and empowered, shiny and insightful space, can cause some trouble and concern. Firstly, because you are so prone to picking up on subtle energy it can cause you to act in ways that are not representative of your true self. To you everything is well and dandy, yet lots of people are projecting negative and distorted vibes and energy towards you; which you pick up on. These subtle influences affect you powerfully! Secondly, some people may actively persecute you or openly judge you for it, which doesn't do great things for your morale and mood. Thus, it is their negativity, delusions or judgements that cause and create the moodiness they believed you to have in the first place. This in itself is a form of "energy vampire" engagement and there are some who will consciously do this to you, judge and persecute you for being empathic. For others, it will simply be an unconscious thing but something which affects you all the same.

Like with the previous point, you need to learn how to speak up and voice your truth. *Singing* can be highly effective on letting others know that you are happy, healthy and upbeat. This can save you from the judgement and resentment of directly telling others how you feel, such as by having to point out that they're suffering from ignorance or disillusionment! For example, why not hum "Bear Necessities" or "Hakuna Matata" when around those who are misperceiving you? Or, let out a loud but natural and authentic laugh! Anything you do to express yourself and show yourself in your divine and inspired light will help you massively, further saving you from misunderstandings and subsequent potential ill-treatment. Don't forget, there are a lot of negative, toxic and narcissistic characters, and many people *do* project their own "stuff" onto you.

THE DAILY STRUGGLES

Expanding on from "Misunderstood Behaviors" … why is it that other people are the ones who judge, act cold or hurtful and are the unmindful and uncompassionate ones, yet you are the one to be misperceived? Well, this question alone is the foundation of your daily struggles. But your daily struggles extend a bit further than this. In this section, we look at three highly significant struggles to the empath personality. Take note, dear empath, because you will most likely suffer from them at some point in your life.

The inability to say "no" (and being taken advantage of)

One of your main issues in life is the inability to say no. Connected to this is the sad but very real truth that you are often taken advantage of, at least until you have grown up and learned to have boundaries. Being taken advantage of is something which occurs when you attract abusers, narcissists and other toxic characters into your energy field. As discussed earlier, your selflessness and compassion is seen as a light, which it is; but unfortunately some people don't want to shine with you- they instead wish to take. You may literally give too much through generous and kind means, or you may be manipulated and fooled by less than pure characters. Honesty, sincerity and purity are values which define and shape you, however they are not qualities which define everyone. It can be very difficult for you to understand and fully accept the coldness and harshness of this world. You truly do have a very pure and gentle heart.

Learning when to say no and when to give is one of your key lessons. Being an empath is one of the most advanced and evolved personality types one could display and embody in this lifetime. There are many people who both believe and recognize that we all have a soul, a timeless and eternal aspect to ourselves. It is spirit which flows through all living things and connects us, further opening us up to qualities such as empathy, compassion and higher awareness or understanding. Yet our souls are our gateways to a higher consciousness, and directly to the empath blueprint.

We have spoken at various points thus far about frequency and vibration, about how empaths operate and exist on a higher frequency. Well, there is great truth in this. Linked to soul is the concept of *karma* and being an empath has a deeply karmic element to it. Karma is the exchange of energy, how our intentions and actions ripple out to affect external environments and our relationships. In essence karma influences everything- the choices we make and ways we behave has a direct influence on our future. But karma is not just limited to linear time or a 3- dimensional reality, we are also profoundly affected by karma from the past, or from past lives. Now, whether you believe in past lives or the timelessness of the soul is irrelevant. The main thing you need to be aware of, as an empath, is that your core essence is unique. Your soul has already gone through many trials and tests to get to the stage it is now, in this life. In order to reach the evolved emotional frequency and psychic or spiritual gifts which accompany, you would have to have evolved. Evolution of the soul is a fundamental part of being. So, being an empath has a strong karmic element because you have reached a level of supreme kindness, selflessness, compassion and understanding. The qualities which make you an empath haven't magiced out of nowhere- you have been on a long journey to get to where you are now and to embody the qualities you do. In this respect, empaths can be seen as the next stage in the evolutionary journey.

This means a core struggle to your unique frequency and persona is to do with your kindness and generosity. It is natural for you to want to give, give and give some more, because this is who you are. You have transcended selfish and lower vibrational ways of being and thinking. Unlike narcissists, for example, you are primarily concerned with authentic connection and helping others, shining sincerity and other beautiful and genuine qualities. Your proneness to always saying "yes" when you should sometimes, in fact, be saying "no" therefore comes with the karma. Your *karmic lesson*, henceforth, is to respect and honor yourself, your time, your gifts and your resources, so that you can live your best life without being depleted.

Intimacy issues: trouble opening up to love and sexual union

Intimacy and sexual love is a major theme and area for considerable learning, growth and transformation. It has already been established that you thrive off connection and have no problems connecting to others on an emotional level, so we won't readdress your strengths further. However, due to operating at such an advanced emotional frequency this can pave the way for fears and issues regarding intimate love, such as in personal relationships and matters of sexual union. You feel very deeply and intensely and this makes you particularly sensitive in personal affairs of the heart. Giving yourself to someone is a massive, life changing and almost spiritual thing and experience. Whereas some can experience sexual union and intimate connection in a very lighthearted and even careless way, for you it is heavy and intense. This is because when you merge- you merge. You give your mind, body, heart and soul, and even if just getting to know someone or connecting on a free-spirited level- which many empaths are capable of- you still tend to "go all in." This may not literally translate as suggesting marriage or declaring your undying love, however it does signify that you invest a lot emotionally. And when we say a lot, we mean A LOT!

Love is intense, feelings are an investment, and sex is more than just a senseless act; it is making love, or at the very least using sexual union as a way to bond and merge. Regarding feelings being an "investment," remember what was shared about there being an integral karmic element to embodying the empath blueprint... From the way you perceive, feel and relate to your potential love interest you naturally give a part of yourself. Now, assuming that you are at a healed, whole and "boundaried" (stage of healthy boundaries) place in your life, giving your time, love and empathy through the time spent and energy exchanged is not something you like to do nor even comprehend doing if dealing with a narcissist. Quite simply, just the thought alone of investing your time and energy into someone who doesn't respect, appreciate or cherish you for the beautiful being that you are is enough to make you close off completely. Speaking from a place of maturity and with awareness to you moving past karmic and toxic relationships, once you get to a certain age and certain stage in your growth cycle if there is even the tiniest of notions that you are, in fact, moving towards intimacy with a narcissistic or toxic character, you instantly put up your barrier (and rightly so!). Of course, when younger and still going through lessons karmic and toxic relationships can be very common, but this is only because you have yet to learn and integrate the wisdom and lessons.

Moving forward from this, it is because of these minor hiccups throughout your love life that intimacy and sex are viewed as very serious to you. You have dealt with toxic relationships and have most likely attracted at least one narcissist into your aura at some point (again, this is speaking from a level of adulthood and maturity, assuming you are in your evolved stages of empathic life). You know what it is like to give your all and put your complete trust in someone, and to have had it broken. The *empath-narcissist dynamic* is an intrinsic part of being an empath and something we explore in depth later. It is also something you will learn if you are not yet in a more mature or older stage in life. Unfortunately, virtually all true empaths attract a narcissist at some stage and further enter into a very unhealthy and difficult relationship.

So referring back to troubles in intimacy and sexual expression and sharing, due to your giving and selfless nature you are prone to being abused, taken advantage of or deeply hurt. When you have your trust broken it can feel like the end of the world, and this is because to you it is- it is the end of your world. Your entire identity is built around the love, kindness, trust and compassion you give others, and this includes your lover or partner. Close bonds and friendships can be equally heartbreaking. You may find from your mid to late twenties or early thirties that "life-long" friends or even certain family members fall out of your life. As much as you are accepting and non-judgemental, their selfish and mean-spirited ways may be too much for your sensitive soul and heart to bare, and you may come to the realization that, as much as they are family or you have known them for nearly all of your life, they are not the people you thought they were. This can be devastating but also open you up to new found strength, self-autonomy and independence. In fact, a self-empowered, independent and self-assertive empath is one of the strongest types of people you could ever meet. There is so much more to be said here but we will cover more on this topic in Chapter 6. All you need to be mindful of in terms of *daily struggles* is that you do not close yourself off to love and intimacy based on past experiences, and that you acquire the discernment, wisdom and awareness to know the difference between a true soulmate or fellow empath on your wavelength, and a narcissist or manipulative toxic character.

Addictions and escapism

Both addiction and escapism are integral to the empath personality and journey. Addictions can take many forms. Alcoholism, excessive t.v. or "screen time," drugs- both recreational and pharmaceutical, food, sex, porn, lust, o.c.d type tendencies, repetitive and unhealthy ways of thinking- any one or all of these may be reocourring themes throughout your life. This is mainly due to your need for emotional connection. It is not new knowledge to learn by now that you operate at a higher emotional frequency than others, and this is confirmed by your unique empathic gifts and abilities. Your tendency to turn towards addiction mostly occurs when you lose sight of your true self and steer away from your essence. When connected to your true self, you are kind, compassionate, self-aware, insightful, perceptive and centered; your boundaries are strong and intact and you have a powerful yet non-invasive assertiveness and strength to you, combined with being self-empowered and content with yourself. Yet the moment you begin to lose touch with your "inner empath" you can start to go down a self-destructive cycle. The various addictions described are the manifestations of this effect.

Addiction serves a temporary and brief purpose- a purpose created as a sort of defense mechanism and safety- net. Your addictive tendencies allow you to go inside yourself and connect to the core of your own being. Of course, no addiction is healthy- and this certainly doesn't do any favors for your empath nature; however it does help you feel safe and secure inside your own reality. Remember that being an empath can be a highly heightened sensory or even spiritual and somewhat mystical/transcendental experience- you feel and conceptualize intensely- so this makes you completely entwined with your emotional frequency and need of connection. When or if the world becomes too harsh or feeling so intently becomes too much to bare, you go inside yourself to save yourself from other people's illusions, or to keep your own sense of personal identity intact. This leads to your other daily struggle, *escapism*.

Escapism for yourself as an empath is exactly as the name implies. To escape is to withdraw, and this also means you may fall into repression and unconsciously or consciously rejecting certain parts of yourself. We all have a shadow self- an inner "darkness" which we often like to deny or repress. But it is through acceptance and integration of the shadow within that we can truly see and embody the light. Escapism and falling into addiction are two ways in which you frequently seek to reject your shadow side, at least until you are whole and healed. Balance is thus very important for you. You may choose to escape into a world of fantasy or make-believe for many reasons but the intention is always the same; to avoid a part or parts of yourself you don't wish to accept. The definition of escapism is *the tendency to seek distraction and relief from unpleasant realities.* Excessive entertainment or addictions, fantasy and day-dreaming are three key routes to achieve this. Yet these aren't healthy and they don't contribute to your brilliant and beautiful empathic nature. Working on your shadow self and attaining greater balance in all areas of your life can help to combat this, significantly. Your shadow is a source of power, of raw and magnificent emotional power, connection and awareness; so it is no wonder that you steer towards escapism when the world becomes too much. Again, your whole sense of worth and identity is tied into your emotional power and connection with others. The shadow self is an embodiment of light and dark, emotion and vulnerability- the places you *thrive* when at your best. Hopefully, you are beginning to see the link between falling into addiction and escapism and losing touch and sight of your empathy and power.

SUCCUMBING TO UNHEALTHY HABITS

You also struggle with repetitive patterns and thought processes which create problems and tensions in daily life. Below is an introduction into these.

1. Happy to heal others, but struggle healing yourself

Your capacity for compassion and empathy is truly admirable. You would be happy to spend hours in mindful and humble service to others, friend and loved one or a stranger in need. Yet do you apply the same love and devotion to yourself? I suggest not! Self-healing is paramount in the journey of an empath and without it you may find yourself falling into negative traps and unhealthy cycles.

How to counter: Spend sufficient time healing yourself through self-care and self-love. Daily massage, nature walks, and gentle activities aid greatly in your emotional well-being. Reading spiritual literature or poetry, listening to motivational and inspiring TED talks, podcasts or documentaries, and engaging in creative and artistic expression can also be gems in your life. Soul-searching and soul work are further particularly effective for the empath nature; they help you attune to your true essence and remind you of your worth, power and greatness. They can also help you to overcome any shadow issues or blocks you may be dealing with.

2. Inability to relax and let go

Surrendering to your journey should be a daily mantra for you as an empath. Your inability to relax fully stems from your need to be an empath. It may sound strange, as an empath is who you are; but the perpetual desire to hold space, be a listening ear or take on the role of a wise counsellor often leaves you with a slight nervous disposition. You may feel anxious, stressed or nervous for no apparent reason, and you further put intense obligations and responsibility on yourself. You feel it is your duty to be the strong one for those you love. This creates a heaviness which can leave you feeling unrelaxed and tense.

How to counter: For you, the best thing you can do is to immerse yourself in creativity. Dance, master a musical instrument, draw, paint, or take up an artistic craft. You can also make use of your imagination. All of these things are great for relaxing and letting go as they connect you to your inner child, the free-spirited and fun-loving aspect of yourself. It is a simple yet powerful route to healing, joy and inner contentment!

3. Weak boundaries

Your weak boundaries will be an issue throughout life until a few different things happen. You will almost certainly deal with at least one narcissist in your life and most likely enter into some unconscious karmic and energetic entanglement with one. You will also attract toxic characters such as as takers and "energy vampires," or at the very least wholly selfish and non-empathic people displaying strong elements of narcissism. Furthermore, you will find yourself suffering or struggling and continuously absorbing everyone else's stuff. This can be problems, illusions, ill- wishes, negative energy, emotions and trauma. You are a psychic and emotional sponge, so expect all the things that come with weak boundaries (until you heal yourself!).

How to counter: Practical aura-strengthening exercises and activities. Work with crystals and special gemstones, as they help to *raise your vibration* and center and ground you. Speaking of grounding, spending time in nature and even walking barefoot (where safe!) are highly effective paths to feeling strong and self-aligned. Nature grounds your energy and enables you to feel connected and secure within your own body, your physical environment, and the world around.

4. Aversion to loud noises and crowded spaces

This may not sound like an unhealthy habit at first

glance, but your strong and deeply ingrained aversion to loud noises and crowded space can create some significantly detrimental habitual responses and reactions. When surrounded by lots of people you can suffer from nervous tension or anxiety. You can also become pulled out of your center, losing your sense of self-alignment and self-autonomy, and with this comes a decrease in confidence. Your self-esteem can become increasingly affected if you do not learn how to center yourself and remain strong in your truth and personal boundaries. The same is true for loud noises- they pull you out of your sense of security and comfort, distracting you and dispelling your energy in various directions.

How to counter: Boundaries are the key here, but so is knowing when is the right time to socialize or go out and when you truly need to spend time alone. Introspective activities are incredibly healing and grounding for you. You also benefit greatly from staying aligned to your own vibe which can be achieved through singing. Why not pick a song that keeps you happy, upbeat and positive with your mind on point, and sing it as you walk through crowded spaces? For me personally, *The Bear Necessities* and *Hakuna Matata* always work!

5. Anxiety and depression?

A lot of empaths experience stages of anxiety and/or depression, especially when young and possibly into young adulthood. Both of these mental disorders are birthed from your capacity to be such an extreme emotional sponge and "dumping ground." You are incredibly sensitive- until you have learned to control and fine-tune your sensitivities this gift will keep resulting in unhealthy patterns and behaviors. You may not suffer from actual depression but instead show depressive tendencies. This is still extremely bad for your health, so learning to overcome anxiety and depression disorders and symptoms will allow your true empath gifts and nature to shine.

How to counter: Read the next chapter!

5

STAY EMPATHIC WITHOUT BURNING OUT

ACCEPT YOURSELF

The notion that empaths are too sensitive is a common theme throughout both your life and the collective societal mindset. Yet, our thoughts hold great power and it is the belief and continual projection that can create the "weight" associated with this belief itself. It is not wrong to be and feel sensitive, nor is it something that you should feel ashamed and guilty for. You also don't have to change who you are or be any lesser to accommodate, or appease, other people. Appeasement and people-pleasing is a key theme throughout your life. Your innate drive and desire to be "everything for everyone" can leave you feeling drained and depleted of energy. Although not a direct form of non-acceptance, this leads to a sort of non-self-acceptance as you literally sacrifice parts of your self and own self-worth and identity to appease or please others. You become 1 hundred different things and versions of yourself to various people, or you could very well fall into the trap of feeling like you have to play chameleon and change your personality accordingly. This can have its benefits, taking on a chameleon-like role can lead to much growth and connection, and further allow you to access your inner empath; but, on the whole, adapting so frequently inevitably makes you lose parts of your true self and personal identity.

Being so adaptable is both a blessing and a curse. With regards to the topic of non-acceptance, however, you need to understand that your self-esteem, strength, self-worth, health and gifts are closely connected to the people around you, or to those you choose to give your time and energy. ***We are all one, interconnected and unified in a subtle way*** is a good thing to be mindful of here. Your empathy is deeply entwined with your emotions and the emotions of those around you. Merged with your inherent pull towards emotional melding and bonding and your genuine desire to use your empathy, to heal, inspire, uplift or provide comfort, your vibratory state of health and well-being affects those closest to you. Let's look at a few examples.

1. You are happy, inspired, positive and upbeat. This actively ripples out to make those around you optimistic and upbeat. You can change the tone or mood of a room or social scenario simply through your own feelings and energy alone. Others around you may become inspired, stimulated or connect to their artistic gifts and creative self in your presence.
2. You are mellow, perceptive and wholly connected to your inner empath. This means that others around you are silently but powerfully influenced. Being in such a receptive and introspective space enables the people around you to be more in tune with their own emotions and femininity. Receptivity and passivity are feminine qualities- and this has nothing to do with

being male or female. The physical manifestations can include others being energized and inspired by changing the topic of conversation or suggesting to watch a compassion-based documentary, or educational video. Or, they may themselves begin to shift and initiate empath-like qualities reflecting into the group dynamics.

Never Ignore the Small Hole in the Boat!

Figure out what drains you, what causes you to burn out and "how many holes there are in your boat." Imagine yourself as a ship sailing gracefully across the sea... The ocean and waters of the world are seen to represent our subconscious, the vast and deep infinite waters where all of our beliefs, identity, thoughts and impressions arise. Our emotions are also birthed from water and emotions themselves are said to be watery in nature, or of the water element. In terms of being equated with a "ship," we enter into relationships everyday, and we also have a relation*ship* with ourselves. We are essentially the masters of our own lives and our own destiny, so recognizing your capacity and capability for steering your own ship, so to speak, is what will allow you to live your best life. You should see yourself as a ship or boat with many lives on board. You are the captain and you are therefore responsible for the people on ship; yet, what happens when there's a hole or many holes? Everyone risks the chance of drowning, of course. One small hole could lead to everyone's demise and could even sink the entire ship.

This may sound extreme but the truth is, as an empath you hold considerable responsibility. Your emotions and mood influence everyone around you. Your subtle intentions radiate outwards to affect the overall mood and "vibe" of the room, gathering or physical environment. Your thoughts, intentions and feelings are powerful and you are connected to everyone through a subtle and invisible realm. But this unseen and "invisible" realm is very real, it shapes, creates and influences physical reality as we know and define it. It is our experiences that are manifested through emotions and the subtle powers of thought and mind. Therefore, embodying such an evolved and supercharged emotional frequency and intelligence means that you are naturally powerful and influential. You don't seek to gain power or control over others, like some narcissistic or overly dominating characters; you do it naturally and almost effortlessly. The power of your mind, heart and emotions are enough to leave those around you feeling loved, comforted and empowered, or low, distorted and less than joyful and optimistically inspired. In short, your mood influences others' moods.

Get Plenty Of "Me time"

Spending time alone is essential for your health and well-being. This is possibly one of the most important and fundamental things to be aware of as an empath, next to the points expressed below in the next section of this chapter. Due to your giving, selfless and helpful empathic nature you frequently find yourself depleted in energy. People and excessive social interactions and situations can drain you, much more so than the average human or extroverted person. You pick up on the thoughts, emotions, subtle impressions and projections of others, and this leaves you feeling drained, depleted and low. You are the fuel to everyone's fire! This is not being spoken from an egotistical, self-delusional or self-absorbed way- the truth is that you are a guiding light, and you further hold the light and energetic frequency of a room or space. Your family may recognize this too and turn towards you, when older, when they need some compassionate and empathic advice. Friends and peers certainly know that you are the one they can always rely on for words of wisdom, and kind and gentle support and a listening ear. But all of this means that you can burn out and give too much of yourself away...

It is only when you are whole and balanced within, with inner happiness and harmony, that your can reflect and project empathy outwards.

Me time is a chance to recharge your batteries and replenish your energy levels. It is only when you are whole and balanced within, with inner happiness and harmony, that you can reflect and project empathy outwards. Spending time alone, eating alone, taking sufficient time for rest and rejuvenation, and setting time for introspection and creative/artistic activities, are the best ways to recharge your batteries and replenish your "inner empath." Remember that your inner empath is a blueprint- a unique and specific coding of information responsible for the way you think, feel and interact with others. How do you expect to be the best version of yourself for others, and heal, inspire and influence through your kindness and compassion, if you are not taking care of yourself? Sacrificing your own needs is not healthy or beneficial for anyone. It is actually extremely detrimental and destructive. So, committing to the things listed are a sure way to success and achieving the personal harmony you deserve and desire.

1. *Spend time alone*: Eat alone, meditate, go for nature walks, watch inspiring documentaries, read, or simply *be* and relax with your favorite music. We are human beings- not human doings, so taking the time to be is incredibly powerful for your energy levels and self-esteem. Creating the belief or mindset that you need to constantly do and engage in mental activity, or perpetually hold and embody a certain emotional frequency for the benefit of others (or the world as a whole, as many empaths do!) is not good for you, to put it simply. It can diminish feelings of self-worth and contribute to the decrease in your self-confidence and self-empowerment. Furthermore, it is through *mindful solitude*; i.e. not succumbing to escapism or self-destructive habits and behaviors, where your light can truly grow

and shine. This then allows you to be an empath for when you do choose to socialize and interact with family, friends or peers.

2. *Take time for rest and rejuvenation*: Go back and read over the daily struggles and unhealthy habits sections of the previous chapter. Create a *vision board* or *mind map* with effective solutions and self-help strategies that will help you to be able to better relax. Also, the self-love and self-care tips in the next section apply directly here.

3. *Introspective activities*: Introspection is very important as an empath. Introspection should not be confused with introversion, however. To be introverted is to be shy and reserved or concerned with one's own thoughts and feelings, as opposed to external environments and situations (and other people). Introspection is a form of self-analysis and examining your own mental, emotional and psychological (or spiritual) processes. Introspective activities, henceforth, help to align you and connect you with your own true essence and self. Soul-searching and spiritual alignment can

be achieved through introspection, as can self-development in many aspects of life.
4. *Immerse yourself in creative and artistic expression*: Everything that was expressed in the first chapter should be remembered and reassessed here. There is nothing more restoring and healing to an empath than creative and artistic self-expression. Your imagination is advanced and fine-tuned, and this means that you should perpetually energize it. Dance, art, photography, craftship, music- do it all dear empath! Creativity energizes your soul and lifts your spirits. It can help to overcome anxiety, depression and any of the daily struggles mentioned previously. It also assists in powering your empath nature as a lot of your empathy is connected to your capacity for ingenious thinking. Your mind and emotions are attuned to a higher frequency, a realm and dimension where subconscious influences and subtle thought forms are rich. You are infinite with infinite potential and creativity is the source of creation.

If ever in doubt, repeat this mantra: *"By giving quality*

time to myself, I am better able to give my time and energy to others. My sensitivities are a strength and a superpower- but only when channeled wisely and when in harmony with my own best interests, needs and wants. Self-love is not selfish, nor is it bad. When I give myself space to shine I allow others to do the same. We are all one and interconnected!"

Self-love is Self-care

Self-love is self-care and self-care is self-love. They are also both self-respect, contributing to your autonomy and growth mindset. It has already been established that you have a healing nature, and a huge part of being an empath lies within your healing capabilities. Many empaths even go on to become intuitive healers, therapists, psychics or spiritual counsellors or guides of some sort. A lot of self-love and self-care has been covered, so in this section we will focus on the power and importance of *diet*. Clean living and healthy eating are the best routes to maintaining your energetic vibration and staying aligned to your empath essence. Because empathy is a state of being and awareness birthed from emotions and emotional connection, drinking lots of water and keeping your physical vessel clean and pure is essential for your well-being, and your ability to thrive as an empath. We are all channels, vessels of consciousness and emotions. For this reason alone, there are certain foods you can incorporate into your diet to help raise your vibration. Let's look at these now.

1. Leafy Greens

Dark leafy greens raise your vibration. They are high in life force, nutrients and water content and can help keep you full while feeling light, simultaneously. They also have a positive effect on your emotions due to being natural and a primary food source. As the mind, body, spirit, and emotions are designed to work in harmony, eating leafy greens will have a profound effect on your emotional and physiological well being as well as your physical and psychological health.

Leafy greens include: Spinach, lettuce, collard greens, arugula (rocket), chard, broccoli, mustard greens and kale.

2. Raw Living Food

Any raw living food such as sprouts and sprouting vegetables are all perfect for your health and emotional well-being. This is because these foods help you develop a connection to spirit and the natural world and keep you functioning at a high emotional frequency. All living things have a spiritual-energetic essence, and vegans and spiritual engagers recognize this. They also enhance your intuition due to the intention of eating foods which are natural and alive. Living raw food also contains the highest amount of natural enzymes. Enzymes help remove toxins from the body, increase digestion and are the essential life-force of food.

3. Avocados

Avocados are loaded with healthy and nutritious nutrients, vitamins and minerals and also contain healthy monounsaturated fats. They have antioxidants which can aid in many bodily functions, such as eye and heart health, and have a positive effect on your well being and perception. The reason why avocado is included here is because of its importance in vegetarianism. As you may have noticed, there are no 'meats' included here. This is because of the intrinsic connection eating animals has to emotional and spiritual awareness and connection. Your cells "'know" and are deeply intelligent. Consciousness runs through your veins and your cells just as it streams through your mind. Avocados have such a rich source of protein and good fats that they can be part of a balanced and healthy, compassionate diet; perfect for your empath nature!

4. *Maca*

Maca is a superfood found in Peru. It provides energy, vitality and sustenance and is high in life force. It is also known to increase sexual vitality and libido, which can be very beneficial for overcoming emotional eating, something often associated with being an empath. One of the main reasons maca is beneficial is due to the stabilizing effect it has on emotions. It can act as a hormonal regulator and balancer and therefore provides both emotional stability, and health and energy and vitality simultaneously. Maca is usually consumed in smoothies or when sprinkled on salads and is often referred to as a superfood.

5. *Walnuts*

There is a reason people call this the brain nut! All nuts are good for keeping your watery-emotional qualities aligned and strong, however walnuts are one of the best. They have an incredible effect on your brain and therefore psychological and mental well being, which intrinsically influences your emotions, and due to the high life force and natural essence of walnuts they can keep you spiritually in tune and perceptive (which positively affects your intuition, which in turn influences your emotional well-being). Walnuts have one of the highest antioxidant compositions of all the nuts, therefore including these in your diet will help to reduce and eliminate any stress associated with dealing with toxic characters like energy vampires and narcissists, or with sensitivity in general.

6. Superfood Smoothies

Superfood smoothies are one of the best ways you can keep your emotional, psychological and spiritual health strong. The best kinds of milk to use are organic and natural nut or dairy-free milks, like hemp, almond, cashew, hazelnut, coconut or soy milk. These can be mixed with a variety of fruits and superfoods. *Chlorella, spirulina, wheatgrass, lucuma, baobab,* and *moringa* (and *maca*) are all foods which should be introduced into your smoothie, as they are all very good for your constitution. They are also high in life force, nutrients and energy and actually aid in emotional connection and awareness.

7. Superfruits

Like superfoods, superfruits are very effective at

helping you thrive emotionally. Superfruits include strawberries, raspberries, blueberries, goji berries, goldenberries, gooseberries, cranberries, and any other berry you come across. They connect you to the natural world and a natural vibration, and are simultaneously high in life force (universal energy). They are pure and can aid in your intuitive and creative abilities due to the natural and water aspect. Water is the source of life and the source of your emotional desires and needs. There are people who live off fruits alone, these people are called fruitarian. Although I am not suggesting you become one, fruitarians are some of the happiest and healthiest people alive!

8. Medicinal Mushrooms

One of the most powerful and health-ful foods for you to consume is medicinal mushrooms. Not only are they high in life force and water content, but they are also strongly linked to other types of mushrooms which help expand your consciousness and see life in a unified, spiritual and interconnected way. Medicinal mushrooms include *Reishi, Oyster, Shitake, Maitake, Lions Mane, Cordyceps*, and *Chaga.* They can be consumed as a tea, eaten, or taken as supplements.

9. Cacao

Cacao is also known as raw chocolate and is extremely good for emotional issues or imbalances. Cacao is rich in antioxidants, high in nutrients and generally makes you feel good. It releases happy endorphins! An interesting thing to know about cacao is that when you drink it, either in a smoothie or as a hot chocolate, the plant leaves its trail on the side of your glass; it *looks like roots*. This shows how high in life force it is, and how consuming it can improve your psychological and spiritual well being. It is a deeply-spiritually stimulating food source, just like superfoods, superfruits, and medicinal mushrooms. Connecting to your inner spirit or soul can, of course, have wonderful effects on your emotional health and the way you feel.

10. Organic or Wholefoods

Any organic or wholefood - a food source which has come from the earth, are perfect for an emotionally-inclined (and imbalanced) nature. When you are looking to make a life-long change and heal from emotional related issues for good, it is very important that you constantly keep in mind your holistic self. A diet is not just a short term fix, a diet is a lifestyle. Beans, pulses, legumes, vegetables, nuts and seeds are all considered wholefoods and can therefore be integrated into your diet for lasting effect. Fish, lean meats and seafood are much better meat choices than red meat, or meat which has been processed in a commercialised way. Factory farms and a lot of the meat sold in Western society has many detrimental health effects. Not only does this affect you physically but it also has severe negative effects on your emotional and mental-psychological health. We explore this more in the next section.

11. Pure and Clean Water

Although it is not food, pure and clean water should arguably be included. This is because one of the fundamental aspects of suffering from emotional eating or addictive tendencies is that emotions are watery in nature- their elemental physiology is water. Consuming too much food, or the wrong types of food, can leave you depleted, emotionally closed off and with a clouded intuition. Water is *healing*, it heals and cleanses the system. Just a 3-day water fast can cleanse and 'detox' the liver and a 7-day water fast can begin cell regeneration, kick-starting your immune system. Besides fasting, water is life force in its purest, and it is the water element that can provide you with such a fine-tuned intuition and sensitivity. If you are ever suffering from heavy emotions or low moods, water can be a game changer. Make sure the water you drink is purified, mountain or spring, and filtered, or even better, reverse osmosis.

"Low Vibed" Foods VS "High Vibed" Foods: Know the Difference!

To be en-'light'-ened is to be aware, intuitive, intelligent, insightful, perceptive, and connected to your own source of spiritual power and knowing. It also means being connected to your body, both aware of the physical body which holds you and the planet that sustains you. Enlightenment inherently involves feelings of lightness and this cannot be when you are feeling heavy or unhealthy! In this respect there is a deep connection between confidence, self-esteem, being empowered and embodying light, and diet, and being an empath. Food is a source of energy- what energy are you filling yourself with? The key to ending emotional addictive eating often suffered does not necessarily lie in calories, food nutrient content, or the amount of exercise you get. The key is in spirituality- your connection to the most powerful vibration on this planet: love. Love is the strongest vibration and love is compassion, a connection to your higher self or mind, and an awareness of the interconnected nature of life. Animals are sentient souls too and not knowing this, or choosing to push this truth aside for a singular human desire such as taste, is what may be preventing you from thriving in self-alignment. Of course, everyone is different- those self-mastered, dedicated and unbelievably committed athletes among us, for example, may require meat due to their *lifestyle*. For the majority of us, however, eating animals may just be an excuse for us not having the strength and willpower to choose a better way.

But, there is more to the story of meat than compassion, sentimentality and spirituality. There is also the reality of chi, life force and the real and intrinsic effect animal consumption has on our mental, emotional and psychological health.

Food Sources and Chi

Chi is the term used to describe the *universal life force energy* which flows through every living thing. It is in the fruits and vegetables we eat, animals, the sun, sea and waters of the world, air and in us ourselves. Chi is invisible but very real. Martial artists, for example, have been aware of chi and its power for thousands of years. Some of the greatest martial artists and kung fu masters get their power and unique abilities solely from their awareness and cultivation of chi. It is the force responsible for core inner strength, a peaceful and clarity infused mind, and the ability to break pieces of wood with a bare hand, or two fingers! Yet, chi is not just synergistic with these incredible gifts. Chi is also responsible for our own confidence, self-esteem, inner self-empowerment and mental and emotional health. When we feel good we generally want to eat less, or only healthy foods we know are good for us. They provide a source of emotional, mental, spiritual and physical nourishment which we could not get from foods full of artificial chemicals and preservatives, high in fats or carbohydrates, or anything which does not contain an active and vibrant life force. This, of course, has a direct and profound influence on your innate empathy.

Food with high life force/ chi:-

- Fruits, vegetables, nuts & seeds.
- Pulses, beans, legumes and grains.
- Organic and whole foods.
- Natural oils like hemp, coconut, flaxseed and olive.
- Herbs and herbal supplements.

- Plant-based, mostly organic vegan foods (all! ~ non-processed)

The 'Primary & Secondary Cycles'

Something which isn't hugely well known are the primary and secondary cycles. This is referring to the amount of chi and direct source energy in the foods we eat. Now, this is not referring to veganism or vegetarianism, or any of the philosophies behind them (although there is nothing wrong with being compassionate!). What this is related to, however, is the hard truth that when we eat organic wholefoods which have come directly from the earth, the food source is in its primary cycle. In other words, the nutrients, vitamins and feel good natural chemicals have come directly from the air, sun, earth and rain. They can be seen to have the *most chi*. Most animals, if we choose to eat them, are in their secondary cycle, they receive their energy from eating crops. Once we consume the animals, therefore, a lot of the nutrients and essentials from plant-based food sources have already been digested and metabolised. Of course, eating animals who are carnivores make our food source tertiary; the food we consume to sustain us has gone through another cycle.

In essence, choosing a diet which has been created solely from the elements of nature and are high in life force mean the best possible vibration for ourselves. All of life can be seen to be measured in terms of vibration, frequency and energy, so consuming food which has suffered extensive trauma, pain and suffering ultimately means that we absorb the frequency and vibration of that trauma, pain and suffering. In other words, whatever the vibration of the food is, the same vibration will be transferred to us when we consume it. This is terribly and severely detrimental to your emotional health and well-being. Could it be that eating too much meat and absorbing the animals' traumas is what is holding you back? Also, perhaps this is why many people who eat excessive amounts of meat are more likely to be angry, impatient and irritable, and cut off from their sense of spiritual awareness. Or, they at least have the potential to be. Eating 'food' which has gone through pain, suffering and trauma before it reaches our mouths inevitably means the trauma becomes stored in the animal's cells. Remember, the mind, body, spirit and emotions are an *interconnected system*. This means that before death all the feelings of fear, pain, neglect, betrayal, trauma and anxiety are projected into the cells of the animal. We then eat this. Do you see the pattern?!

Energy, Frequency & Vibration: "Mood Food"

You are now aware that the body is a complex and holistic system. You may also have heard of "mood foods." When we eat food high in life force with a good energetic frequency (chi, natural energy, high vibration) we feel good. Positive neurons are transmitted and tell our bodies and our minds that we are feeling healthy, happy and content. There is a strong sense of harmony, well-being and emotional satisfaction. When we eat foods high in sugar we ultimately become depressed. Sugars provide a temporary high, yet it is an unstainable one. It ironically creates low blood sugar levels- as you are not receiving your glucose naturally from fresh fruits and the like - and therefore makes you feel low, moody, irritable, unhappy and unsatisfied, and many other negative feelings and emotions. It also contributes to low self-esteem and low confidence. Lean or natural proteins, complex carbohydrates and pure food sources of your essential vitamins, minerals and amino acids are the best diet combination. There is a reason why "Happy Hens" produce *happy eggs*. The chickens who have produced these eggs have been given freedom to run around and spend time in a natural environment.

The truth is, clean eating and healthy living directly affects the way you live and interact as an empath. You are extremely sensitive and these sensitivities are not exclusive or limited to other people's emotions or feelings. Foods, chemicals, preservatives and the energetic frequency of a food source are all powerful in your strength and soaring, and your demise.

Set Healthy Boundaries

Boundaries is your new power word! Being an empath is hard due to your heightened sensitivity and higher frequency emotional connection and functioning. One of your main issues in life, therefore, is to develop and make friends with the word boundaries. It may be difficult at first, especially due to your innate desire to be "everyone's friend in need" and help others in some way; yet, as you know, this leaves you drained and lacking in energy, vitality and wellbeing. One of the key pieces of wisdom to be aware of when learning about your boundaries is the recent discoveries of neuroscience and quantum physics. Neuroscientists and quantum physicists have found that we are in fact governed by an aura, an electromagnetic energy field which emits, transmits, and receives thoughts, emotions, and subtle impressions. Our auras- or electromagnetic fields- interact with others, and this is not just limited to other humans. Every living thing from plants to flowers and crystals or rocks have an auric field. This means we essentially *converse* with others on a subtle level in every moment of now. This has some profound implications. Emotions, subtle energy and unique spiritual-energetic gifts define empathy, therefore being aware of the power of your own being can be heaven or hell- literally. This is where boundaries come into play.

As you will see later narcissists and other toxic personalities are magnets to your vibe. They simply love your energy, love, compassion, and inner beauty but not in a healthy way. This means that having healthy boundaries and centeredness is *essential*. One of the most effective things you can do is to engage in aura strengthening and developing exercises and activities.

Aura protection exercises

One of the most powerful (and loving) things you could do for yourself is to protect your aura. To some, these techniques may seem slightly 'woo' but spirituality and metaphysics are a fundamental part of life. Many of the people who are living their dream lives, healthy, abundant, and happy with a strong inner focus and protection and genuine love for life are those who are in tune with their spirituality. Aura protection exercises, therefore, will steer you effectively on the journey to healing and wholeness- and overcoming and sabotaging or destructive thoughts or behaviors.

- ***Work with Crystals.*** Crystals embody certain energetic frequencies which can interact with our energy fields for a desired effect. Crystals, therefore, are extremely powerful when wishing to strengthen your aura, protect yourself and develop healthy boundaries. Let's look at three main crystals which can help you in everyday life.

Black Tourmaline: Black tourmaline is specifically referred to as the protection stone. It is grounding, provides a sense of security and trust, and shields you from any 'dark,' harmful, or negative energy. Connecting to this stone can help you feel stronger inside and increase a sense of confidence. Meditating with, connecting to, and simply wearing a black tourmaline bracelet, pendant, or necklace will literally shield you from unwanted energy and interaction (just remember that we use quartz crystals to power watches!).

Amethyst: Amethyst is particularly effective in protecting your aura as it increases your sense of intuition and *inner knowing*. Amethyst is purple and has a majestic feel. It, therefore, can enhance your perception, connect you to your higher mind and inner knowing, and aid in mental clarity in strength when dealing with unsavory characters or situations. Amethyst can act as a psychic shield against negative or harmful energy, therefore, protecting yourself. Again, this crystal can be worn as jewelry or carried around as an individual stone.

Hematite: Hematite is another grounding stone as is helps absorb negative energy and protect your energy field. It can enhance confidence, increase your ability to transform negative situations into positive ones and can calm the mind when responding to stress, anxiety, or worry. Hematite also has an effect on the physical body by its electromagnetic effect on the cells. It can aid in detoxification and strengthen the liver and blood, therefore, enabling you to better protect yourself. Hematite can be carried around and held and connected to for protection and strength in destructive situations.

- ***Self-hypnosis.*** Self-hypnosis is similar to working with crystals in that your magnetic energy field is strengthened and protected. However, with self-hypnosis it is your mind having a direct effect as opposed to crystals. You can literally rewire and restructure your mind (through neurological activity, belief, and thought patterns and reconditioning) which can then act as a tool to shield you from harmful energy. Everything can be seen to start in the mind as the mind is the root of all problems, concerns, solutions, and manifestations of recovery. Self-hypnosis can be performed through many means such as mental reprogramming, mantras, meditation, focused mindfulness, sound therapy, binaural beats and music, reiki and energy healing, and making a conscious effort daily to realign your thoughts and inner focus. You can also see a professional hypnotherapist and gain insights and directions through someone experienced in their field. The key is to remember the power of your mind and to be aware of any unconscious or subconscious beliefs that may be limiting your perspective and holding you down. Once these perspectives are released, your ability to protect yourself through the mind, intention, and thought alone will become clear and amplified. You can also amplify your empathic gifts through the connection self-hypnosis brings to the subconscious.

- ***Connect with nature***. Connecting with nature is possibly one of the most effective ways to protect yourself and strengthen your inner boundaries. Nature connects us to all that is, expands our minds, brings mental focus and clarity, heals emotions, releases wounds and traumas, increases our sense of self and therefore confidence, and generally leads to an enhanced and improved way of being. Developing a special relationship with the elements can really help in your ability to remain strong and centered within and to put up better boundaries.

Just like physical boundaries, *mental boundaries* are extremely important. Have you ever been out and about or in social settings around new people and have begun to feel strange, anxious and on edge? A nervousness took hold, you felt like you couldn't be yourself and that your mind had to protect itself... yet, you couldn't explain it? This is because you are highly sensitive to other people's subtle thoughts and intentions. Even if someone's energy is a bit "off," you will pick up on it. You may sense that although this person is friendly, outgoing, and liked in a social situation, there is some facade or falseness going on. Or perhaps they have some very unhealthy, destructive and harmful beliefs and opinions constructing their energy field.

The best way to deal with this and thrive in the process is to develop strong mental boundaries. You can do this in a number of ways, such as through brain training and strengthening exercises, techniques and activities to enhance your intuition and psychic ability or spiritual perception, and further through working with special gemstones and divinatory objects. Divination is essentially connecting to some natural object or entity which increases your connection to the divine. There is nothing supernatural about it, but it is *super*natural (positive associations only!).

The first way to help protect your mind and strengthen your mental boundaries is by working with special gemstones or crystals. Science has shown that crystals can be used to have a number of positive effects and quartz crystals specifically have been used to power watches due to the electromagnetic effect and connection to the natural world. Ancient Egyptians and many other ancient cultures were aware of the power of rare gemstones in their healing abilities and many people today are becoming increasingly more knowledgeable and increasingly less ignorant as to their healing powers. The other main method to help with mental boundaries as an empath is to engage in daily *meditation and mindfulness* exercises. Meditation and mindfulness are two of the most profound ways to enhance your sense of self, remain confident and aligned/centered, and live your life free from external disruption or harm. As an empath who is naturally in tune with some spiritual, subtle, or subconscious aspect of reality, you may not require the science behind meditation and mindfulness. This is because you learn from experience, you actually feel the beauty, bliss and wonder from connecting to your inner being and mental powers from meditation. For the purpose of balance, however, let's explore some of the scientific studies showing the power of meditation and mindfulness.

Meditation

- A study by *Psychosomatic Medicine Journal of Biobehavioral Medicine* found that mindfulness meditation positively affects brain and immune functioning, specifically increasing positive emotions. [1]
- Research from the *American Psychological Association* discovered that meditation improves positive emotions and enhances loving-kindness.[2]
- Another study shared in the American Psychological Association shows how meditation increases social connection and emotional intelligence. [3]

Mindfulness

- Research published in *Cognitive Therapy and Research* (Volume 28 Issue 4) shows how mindful meditation helps to overcome depression. [4]
- A mindfulness experiment conducted by *Stanford University* discovered that

mindfulness for compassion cultivation works. [5]

In truth, there are too many studies to mention however they all fundamentally show the power and effects of mindfulness and meditation on enhancing the self and improving life in some way. Of course, as an empath, you probably already knew all of this! This is the beauty of your gift.

Practice Grounding

Grounding is almost as important as having healthy boundaries. Walking barefoot on grass, sand or soil connects your energy to Mother Earth's, directly to the life force of our planet. It is healing, rejuvenating and restoring. There is also a powerful tree meditation you can use daily or weekly to re- align and re-harmonize your energy. The meditation below will help to center and ground you, further enabling you to protect yourself in harmful or negative situations. Your sensitivities can be transformed into a super-power instead of a burden. Your empathy will also be fine tuned immensely.

Tree Meditation for inner grounding

Visit your favorite nature spot or a local park or

field. Find somewhere quiet or somewhere you feel comfortable. Find a tree with strong roots and a big trunk and sit down with your back straight, gently resting against the trunk with your knees bent with your feet on the ground. It is best to perform this barefoot as being barefoot grounds your energy with the earth. (Think of chi and life force!) Close your eyes and focus on your breath. Take note of all the sensations around you, the sounds, smells (hopefully of nature), physical sensations and your connection to this strong and ancient tree. Bring your awareness within while still remaining conscious of your surroundings. Once you are calm, peaceful and centered within with an acute awareness of both your physical body and surroundings, try this.

- As you breathe in, visualize a white or golden light being equated with your breath. Watch it travel up your body from your feet to the top of your head and back down again. Do this for 8-10 deep breaths until you feel it starts to come naturally.
- Next, visualize that same white or golden light traveling up the trunk of the tree, from its roots all the way up to the top of its leaves

and back down again. Visualize this happening to the tree as you breathe.

- Finally, synchronize your breath, the visualization of energy traveling through and up yourself and back down again, and the visualization of energy traveling up the tree from the roots to leaves and back down into the earth into one. Merge the individual parts into *synergy* and feel the energy flow through both you and the tree as one.

This exercise is very powerful for grounding yourself, gaining inner strength and chi and protecting your energy. The effects can be used in a number of circumstances and specifically, will aid in how you respond to and interact with toxic people, use your empathic and intuitive gifts, and regain your confidence psychologically and spiritually. It can be performed daily or on a cyclic basis.

Creating a Chi Ball

Creating a chi ball can be used in any situation, at any time. It is essentially using your mental powers and focused intention to expand and develop the natural chi within and around, and grounding it into an energy ball. This ball of chi can then be used to recharge and re-energize any aspect of yourself. Chi, as you may be aware, is the universal life force which flows through every living thing. For example, say you are starting to feel fear or nervous tension in a situation due to your empathic sensitivity. You can take a few minutes to close your eyes, become at peace with yourself and 'charge up' an energy ball, and then place it over your heart or stomach (your stomach is your sacral chakra, which is often where tricky, painful, or fear-based emotions arise). If you ever start to lack insight, you can create a chi ball for your intuition and third eye chakra. If you are starting to question yourself, experience old patterns of low self-esteem or confidence issues through absorbing too much information, the chi ball can be created for your heart chakra. The key is to know that this ball of energy can be created at any time or in any place as the universal life-force energy is always available!

To create your chi ball, visualize a beautiful golden light growing inside your palm chakras. Synchronize your breathing, focus your intention, and really feel this ball of divine energy growing and expanding for your benefit. It is a very effective exercise to incorporate into daily life and can be used to enhance empathy, sight, intuition and any imaginative, creative and intellectual gifts.

Key points:

- Can be used at any time or place.
- Only takes a few minutes.
- Can be used for any intention or to enhance any quality lacking.
- Visualize a glowing ball of beautiful light expanding in between your hands...
- Breathe into the chi ball and watch it grow.
- Place it over any one of your chakras for the desired healing effect!

Learning to Laugh

As an empath, it can be very easy to take life too seriously. Because you are used to feeling appreciated and loved for your wise insights, warm and gentle nature and empathic gifts (once you have grown up and found those who appreciate you), there is a tendency to forget to balance serious, deep and soul-level sharing and connection with *letting go and lightening up.* One of the main reasons you suffer when around people or out of your comfort zone is due to your *oversensitivity*; there really is no need to be so sensitive or self-conscious all the time!

So, to help with this here is a handy tip: *just learn to laugh*! Not a weird, mean or spiteful laugh (you may know *we are all one* and have a strong heart, but not everyone does). But I am referring to a real, sincere and open laugh, a laugh which recognizes your oneness in a situation.

Everyone is a reflection of you; we are all mirrors and sometimes what is truly needed to release trapped emotions and blocked energy is a genuine, deep and real laugh. This can be very helpful in many social situations and help you to take things easy. Combined with the powerful energy exercises, you should find any feelings of anxiousness, tension or low self-esteem disappear in no time. Literally! When you laugh, you release trapped energy and *rise* it to conscious light. A lot of what its stored is unconscious or residing in our subconscious; therefore, in terms of being an empath, your lack of boundaries and letting harmful or negative energy in may arise from not being aware that you are holding on to thoughts or emotions which are not yours. Laughing shakes things up, and subsequently enables you to see and feel your own energy.

Working With Your Dreams or the Subconscious

Looking to your subconscious and in particular your dreams can aid greatly in your ability to develop stronger boundaries and enhanced energy in daily life. As already stated you are a natural dream explorer, whether that be lucid dreaming or exploring the dreamworlds at will (consciously). It is in dreams where you have access to your subconscious, and, specifically as an empath, you are better able than most to tune in to some subconscious message or universal symbolism for healing and insight. This can affect you in so many ways and on so many levels. Any issue you may be suffering with such as oversensitivity, self-esteem or confidence issues, boundaries, problems with speaking your truth, and stepping fully into your light can be overcome and healed through allowing and being open to receive the wisdom inherent within your subconscious. You are intelligent as well as intuitive and your cells "know," they are conscious and aware. It is in dreams where a part of you becomes triggered, activating some aspect of yourself which is currently in the dark.

Other ways to connect to your subconscious include journaling, writing, expressing yourself through art therapy or music, and psychoanalysis or any holistic therapy. Holistic therapy is important for your nature, as being an empath is a *holistic experience*. You are not just three-dimensional!

Developing Discernment

Finally, one of the best ways to get in touch with your superpowers and live your best life is to develop discernment. Now as an empath this may be hard as you are such a giving and selfless soul, yet as you are aware this can leave you depleted and victim to the abuse and will of energy vampires, narcissists, and other toxic personalities. Fundamentally, discernment comes through your intuition and advanced emotional wisdom. You can only access this, however, by being true to yourself and connecting to your unique spiritual and psychically geared gifts. Being an empath inherently involves a psychic and spiritual element, as empathy is literally feeling other people's emotions and feelings and, in more advanced cases, reading others' minds. Again, we are all connected on a subtle level and empathic power is on the same wave as this. There are many ways to develop discernment and hopefully the techniques and exercises shared throughout these chapters can help you do so.

1. https://journals.lww.com/psychosomaticmedicine/Abstract/2003/07000/Alterations_in_Brain_and_Immune_Function_Produced.14.aspx
2. https://psycnet.apa.org/record/2008-14857-004
3. https://psycnet.apa.org/record/2008-13989-015
4. https://link.springer.com/article/10.1023/B:COTR.0000045557.159
5. http://ccare.stanford.edu/article/enhancing-compassion-a-randomized-controlled-trial-of-a-compassion-cultivation-training/

RELATIONSHIPS, CAREER AND WORLD TRANSFORMATION

AN INTRODUCTION

*I*n my second book to this "Empath Series" we explore this topic in depth. We cover empath careers, stepping into a leadership role within your communities and society as a whole, and all aspects of relationships- including toxic characters and how to stay clear of them! For now, however, we will look at the fundamentals of what you need to know.

Why Empaths can be the best friend you could have

1. You are compassionate and selfless. You feel

what is beyond the surface and what is hidden, and this makes you a gem to your loved ones. You often offer guidance and advice and "pull out" aspects of others including physical ailments and inner turmoil. You can raise other people's light significantly, and further do so without judgement or ego. You really are the best friend one could wish for.

2. You possess the unique ability to forgive. Regardless of how much pain or wrong someone has caused you, your empathy knows no bounds. Your whole personality and essence is entwined with your desire to help others and to further transcend pain and suffering. Whereas it is human nature to be primarily selfish and instinctual, seeking to serve one's own needs and succumb to a "survival" and flight or fright/fight or flight response and of course, you will never do this. You are as pure as they come!

3. You put others needs above your own, are happy to give your last pound or item of food, and holistically seek to make everyone's life better. You raise others' spirits and moods through your giving and

genuine nature. Others feel safe, secure and loved around you, and they know that they can count on you. You are a gem and a rock.

Empaths in Love Relationship

- You are a romantic. As a lover, you are sweet, giving and wholly loving. Your compassionate and selfless nature projects into your intimate partnerships, so much so that you may often gravitate towards self-sacrifice. This can be a positive and kind gesture but it can also be detrimental to both your own growth and to the health of the relationships.
- Your partner is an extension of yourself. When you give yourself you give yourself completely. You are also one of the few types of people who believe in and embody the soulmate love. Karma and transcending it is integral to your life path and journey as an empath, therefore to remain in karmic or toxic relationships is not acceptable. Once you get to a certain stage in your evolutionary journey, your relationships begin to operate in the highest frequency

possible. Through raising your own vibration, you raise the vibration of your partnership. You also stop attracting energy vampires, narcissists and other toxic personalities!

- Referring back to romance, like your star sign equivalent *Pisces* you are the old souls of the zodiac. Pisces are often equated with empaths as they embody all of the empath qualities and traits. Learning about the star sign Pisces, therefore, can help you to better understand your own behaviors and yearnings in love. You are soulful, spiritually-inclined and deeply impressionable. Your sensitivities are a gift and your ability to merge and mold can open you up to the most transcendental and blissful sexual unions.
- Your intuition is so strong that it allows you to navigate life's waters with ease, reflecting into the types of relationships you choose. You seek a lover and life partner on your wave. They must be an empath or capable of empathy, and they need to be kind, sincere and sweet too. Cold, harsh or narcissistic and aggressive characters are a

big turn off for you; you don't do well with harshness!

In my next book we cover: *How to thrive as an empath in romantic and intimate relationships, how to thrive in business partnerships, what to avoid in romantic partnerships, how to overcome misunderstandings and miscommunication, the dos and don't in love, how your sensitivities and emotionalism may damage your relationship, self-development techniques and tips, how to succeed and thrive in love, and your most beautiful and essential qualities which further make you one of the best lovers and partners around.*

Empaths, be wary of narcissists

Narcissists are selfish, emotionally abusive and manipulative. They gravitate to your light like a moth to a flame... Everything that should be honored and cherished is not, your kindness and sincerity is seen and treated as weak. At first, a narcissist will charm you and make themselves appear as a kind, charismatic, friendly and loving character, yet once you get to know them and let them into your personal space; things begin to change.

In my next book we cover: *The origin of narcissism,*

Narcissistic Personality Disorder (NPD), the empath- narcissist dynamic and dance, other toxic characters and your interactions with them, how to recognize such people, how to shield yourself from their bs, how to practice self- love and recover from narcissistic abuse, the "red flags" in dating and early friendship, letting go of toxic love, what to look for in your new partnership, karmic love VS soulmate love, and how and why interacting with an extreme narcissist is often essential for your growth & evolution (and how to learn from it!).

The empath's role in society and the world at large

Being empathic means that you have a larger role to play. Your empathy and associated gifts are so powerful that it would be devolving to not live up to them. Your whole identity and nature is intrinsically bound to your heart- you live with heart and integrity. This signifies that you naturally have a karmic element to your life path and purpose. In other words, you are here to heal and help raise humanity's vibration. This leads us to pose the following question. Is it the unconscious collective, our wounds, traumas, conditioning and collective experiences, which create the empath? Or is it the powerful, loving and unique empathic ways which shape the collective? It would be ignorant to misperceive that being born with such a unique gift has no purpose, or that you should shy away from your true nature. So, in relation to the question, the best way to explore this topic, therefore, is to look to the intention, the why and what this means. Without heart there would be no life; everything in the universe exists because of the vibrational frequency of love. Life is love; creation is love and the earth herself is loving, beautiful and abundant. The empath nature embodies this love.

As briefly explored, the empathic nature can be defined by the heart center- it is essentially its embodiment. Kindness, care, and compassion; a love for mother earth and the natural world, and a deep-seated empathy is intrinsic to the essence of the heart center. As the heart is the center, connecting both our *lower self* and *higher self*, it can be seen that the empath is the perfect representation of this. Empaths are the perfect balance and unification of the lower self, emotions, a deep connection to the earth and all its inhabitants, feeling and birthing new ideas, insights and high power into the physical; and the higher self, intuition, connecting to spirit and unseen realms, dreams and an evolved emotional frequency. In relation to this question, it can be seen that empaths both influence and affect the collective conscious and global energy field, and are a physical manifestation of it. The empath nature is literally to *tune in* and connect to something which is above and beyond the human ego and 'I' centered reality. Arguably, the ultimate way the collective can be seen (in its ideal form) is as an embodiment of love, unity, divinity and conscious global humanity.

Thus, through the empath's intentions, ways, beliefs and actions they actively reshape and restructure the world, and our subsequent collective conscious energy field. ***You actively reshape and restructure the world through your love and compassion***. The beautiful gift of empathy and all its real-life implications and applications enable empaths all over the world to have a powerful effect and be catalysts for love, self-development, healing and evolution, and enhanced gifts of compassion and creative expression. You are love in embodiment!

AFTERWORD

Empathy is a beautiful gift. You are kind, perceptive, compassionate and selfless, and generally possess an advanced level of emotional wisdom, maturity and intelligence. You also have a unique gift for perceiving things beyond the surface, verging on psychic or telepathic ability. Your desire to give, heal and help in whatever way you physically can knows no bounds.

Hopefully, the wisdom, information and techniques in this book will help you to understand your empathy and put up the healthy boundaries necessary to survive and thrive as an empath. The world is not all sunshine and rainbows- there are some deeply toxic and cold characters out there! Narcissists, for one, get massively attracted and drawn to your kind, sincere and gentle nature. They seek to take where you live to give. This is *not* good for your health or beneficial for anyone.

Through developing discernment, learning how to let go, be at ease and lighten up, and developing the inner strength and boundaries necessary to both survive psychologically and thrive; you can start to live your life with grace, higher awareness and the abundance and prosperity you deserve. Being a martyr is not healthy nor is relevant in this day and age. The empath nature is arguably the next stage in human evolution, and hopefully the perspectives inherent throughout these chapters have made it clear why. You are soulful, caring, considerate and cooperative. You are compassionate, wise, intuitive and artistic. You possess the gifts and abilities to be an inspiring poet, writer, mystic, philosopher, musician, healer, therapist or counsellor. You also have a deeply spiritual side, even if you do not choose a conscious spiritual path. All of this makes you a pretty amazing human being!

So, don't live in self- denial and do not shy away from your gifts. Certainly don't repress or reject core and essential aspects of yourself that make you who you are. If I, speaking as your reflection, subconscious and higher self, wish to learn anything from this book it would be to develop and integrate the self-acceptance and self-compassion necessary to flourish in this lifetime. *Your* self-care, self-love and self-empowerment take priority above everyone's else's. Never forget this.

Please stay tuned!

If you have enjoyed this book, you will almost certainly enjoy my next one. In the second empath book we delve into romantic relationships, platonic, sexual and business partnerships, energy vampires and narcissists, letting go of toxic characters, the empath's role in society, best careers for an empath, how and when to step into leadership, empaths in society, the empath as the humanitarian and idealist, the rewards of being an empath in both this New Age and the modern world, and a deep exploration of how to work with your subconscious and universal archetypes, as advocated by profound psychologists and psychoanalysts, for healing, wholeness and self- discovery.

REFERENCES

https://journals.lww.com/psychosomaticmedicine/Abstract/2003/07000/Alterations_in_Brain_and_Immune_Function_Produced.14.aspx

https://psycnet.apa.org/record/2008-14857-004

https://psycnet.apa.org/record/2008-13989-015

https://link.springer.com/article/10.1023/B:COTR.0000045557.15923.96

http://ccare.stanford.edu/article/enhancing-compassion-a-randomized-controlled-trial-of-a-compassion-cultivation-training/

CPSIA information can be obtained
at www.ICGtesting.com
Printed in the USA
BVHW090100240421
605637BV00006B/1128

9 781989 838877